There are five titles in the 'Get Going With Creative Writing' series:

All About Me – 978-1-907733-13-0

Likes and Dislikes – 978-1-907733-14-7

Out and About – 978-1-907733-15-4

We Love Animals – 978-1-907733-16-1

What We Do – 978-1-907733-17-8

Guinea Pig Education
2 Cobs Way
New Haw, Addlestone
Surrey
KT15 3AF
Tel: 01932 336553
Website: www.guineapigeducation.co.uk

© Copyright 2012

NO part of this publication may be reproduced, stored or copied for commercial purposes and profit without the prior written permission of the publishers.

ISBN: 978-1-907733-17-8

Written: Sally A Jones and Amanda C Jones
Illustrations: Sally A Jones
Graphic Design: Annalisa Jones

Dear Kids,

Have fun learning to write with our 'Get Going With Creative Writing' series. Enjoy reading our short stories; some which have been written by kids of your age. Use our ideas to write your own stories or try some non-fiction writing, such as, diaries, reports and leaflets. If you read or write well you will achieve high grades at school, so we challenge you to learn to love writing. You just need a notebook and pencil to start working through your guinea pig writing guide. Don't forget to colour in the pictures.

....

Dear Teachers and Parents,

If your children think writing is dull, give them a guinea pig writing book from the 'Get Going With Creative Writing' series and we think they'll change their minds. However, these books are also ideal for those children who love to write, providing starting points that will make any budding young writer's imagination run wild especially if they are preparing for 11+ exams.

We have put together a series of themed books to inspire your child to write at his or her level. Whether you choose 'About Me', 'We Love Animals', 'Likes and Dislikes, 'Out And About' or 'What We Do', you will, choose an English study book with a light-hearted, modern approach to appeal to the children of today.

The books can be used at home or in school alongside existing schemes. Inside, you will find a treasure trove of ideas for writing, featuring fiction and non-fiction themes. Based on the National Curriculum, they comply with the national strategy for literacy, with tips on planning and writing techniques, sentence construction, grammar tips and more.

Written by a former class teacher, working as a tutor, the books have been trialled by the children the author teaches in Surrey. These children agree the books are fun and help them learn to love writing.

> **We would like to thank the students of Guinea Pig Tuition – class of 2010/2011 – Sophia, Georgina, Harriet, Hannah, Sacha, Harry, Gareth, Rahan, Neena, Mahir, Neesha, Jai, Alexandra, Anna Maria and Vlad.**

A French CIRCUS Comes to Town

On holiday, Sam sees a poster for a circus. Although it is written in English, it is difficult to read, because it has no capital letters or full stops.

Rewrite the poster and put in capital letters and full stops.

on market square, antibes, france
from september 4th - 8th, at 7.30pm

come and watch our sensational show with the funniest clowns we also have an incredible trapeze artist, called daring di she will amaze you as she swings on the high wire you will also be thrilled by the leaping lions tickets are 4 pounds for children and 6 pounds for adults

Complete the poster:

THE BIG TOP COMES TO TOWN

Introducing

SEE OUR SENSATIONAL SHOW

Where will you find us?

....

MARKET SQUARE ANTIBES

Including:

- DARING DIAA dangling on a high wire.
- CLEVER TREVOR, the juggler, performing tricks never seen before.
- ....
- ....
- ....
- Lions leaping through hoops will keep you on the edge of your seat.

TUE 4 SEP TO **SAT 8 SEP**

BOOK NOW!

TICKETS COST:

Circle:
Child £ ...., Adult £ ....

Ringside:
Child £ ...., Adult £ ....

WHAT TIME IS THE SHOW?
.... AM/ PM

ADVANCE BOOKING AT THE CIRCUS.

A THRILLING SHOW NOT TO BE MISSED

Let's introduce Claudette and her family.

"Hi, I'm Claudette. I'm nine years old and I travel round with the circus that my parents own. I have a brother called Jean Paul and a sister called Fleur.

We live in a huge caravan which is very luxurious inside. We visit all the cities in Europe to do our shows. I have a tutor who teaches me, but I am also training to be a trapeze artist and a bareback rider. My brother is training to be an acrobat."

She writes in the first person.

"Hi, I am Jean Paul. I am Claudette's brother. I have another sister who is called Fleur. I am thirteen years old and my sisters are aged eleven and nine.

We travel around Europe with our circus. I am learning to be an acrobat which means I have to practise for three hours a day.

We have four hours of lessons a day with our tutor in our caravan. I am doing well in maths, English and music and I'm learning to play the trumpet."

- I am Claudette *(a simple sentence)*

- We live in a circus caravan and it is very luxurious inside *(a compound sentence)*.

- If I practise three hours a day, I will learn to be an acrobat *(a complex sentence)*.

Read and write about Claudette...

Draw Claudette

- This is .... who is ....
- Her parents own .... so ....
- She has a brother .... and a sister ....
- Their home is a .... which is ....
- In the circus she is training to be ....
- Instead of going to school, she has ....
- Claudette's family don't have ordinary pets, they have a ....
....

Read and write about Jean Paul...

Draw Jean Paul

- Claudette's brother is called ....
- He is also the brother of ....
- His age is ....
- Jean Paul is training to be an ....
- so he practices for ....
- A tutor teaches .... for ....
- The musical instrument he is learning to play is ....

You will write in third person (he, she, they)
It is in present tense, so it is happening now.

Jean Paul says, "We have our own zoo at the circus. What animals do we have?"

Match the sentences to the most suitable ending.

Gorgeous white horses	rolls over to have his tummy tickled.
A stripy tiger	gallop fast.
Eight leaping lions	swing their trunks.
Three huge grey elephants	shakes paws with his trainer.
A black panther	leap through hoops with their tails in the air.

(Arrow drawn from "Gorgeous white horses" to "gallop fast.")

Lets Learn English:

The **SUBJECT** is the person who is spoken about.

The **PREDICATE** is the action part of the sentence and has a verb.

ADJECTIVES describe: huge, grey

NOUNS name: elephants, panther

VERBS are action words: roll, gallop, swing, shake, leap

Joining words are called **conjunctions** or **connectives**. They join two clauses to make a compound or complex sentence.

Make up fourteen more animal sentences, using the connectives in bold print below.

The wild cats live in cages	**unless** they are training.
It is time for the lions to perform in the ring	**so** they line up like a group of school children, with their tails held high. (Are they better behaved?)
They bound back to their cages	**as** the show is over.
They roar loudly	**because** they are hungry.
The lions are quiet	**while** they eat a juicy dinner of raw meat.
You will get bitten	**if** you put your hand into the cage.
The zoo opens	**whether** it is good weather or not.
The elephants are gentle	**although** they are big.
There is a small admission cost to get into the zoo	**but** it is only 5 euros.
The animals like Claudette's Granny	**because** she talks to them in French.
It is dangerous to get close to wild animals.	**so** it is only the trainer who is allowed to stroke them.
The lions are tame	**while** they are with granny.
You can peer through the bars	**and** get a view of the cats.
Since she helps train them,	Granny has a name for each lion

Try starting your sentence with a connective.

Meet Claudette's family. They all work in the circus. Match the people to the job you think they might do.

Match the **SUBJECT** to the **PREDICATE**.

Claudette	Jean Paul	Fleur
Claudette's Mum, Sophie	Claudette's Dad, Pierre	Claudette's Auntie, Francine
Claudette's Uncle, Simon	Claudette's Granny, Arlette	Claudette's Cousin, Dominique

trains lions and talks to them.	is a bare back rider.	checks tickets and shows people to their seats.
takes ticket money and helps people choose a seat.	is a clown with bright red lips.	is learning to be an acrobat.
leads in the tiger on a rope.	is the ring master in top hat and tails.	is training to be a trapeze artist.

Let's Visit Claudette's Circus

Sophie, says,

- "Look at the plan of the big top. Choose seats for your friends and family. (*I would like...*)

- Pick a date and time for the show you would like to attend. (*on... at...*)

- How many seats would you like for adults and how many for children? (*I need... adults... children*)

- It will cost..."

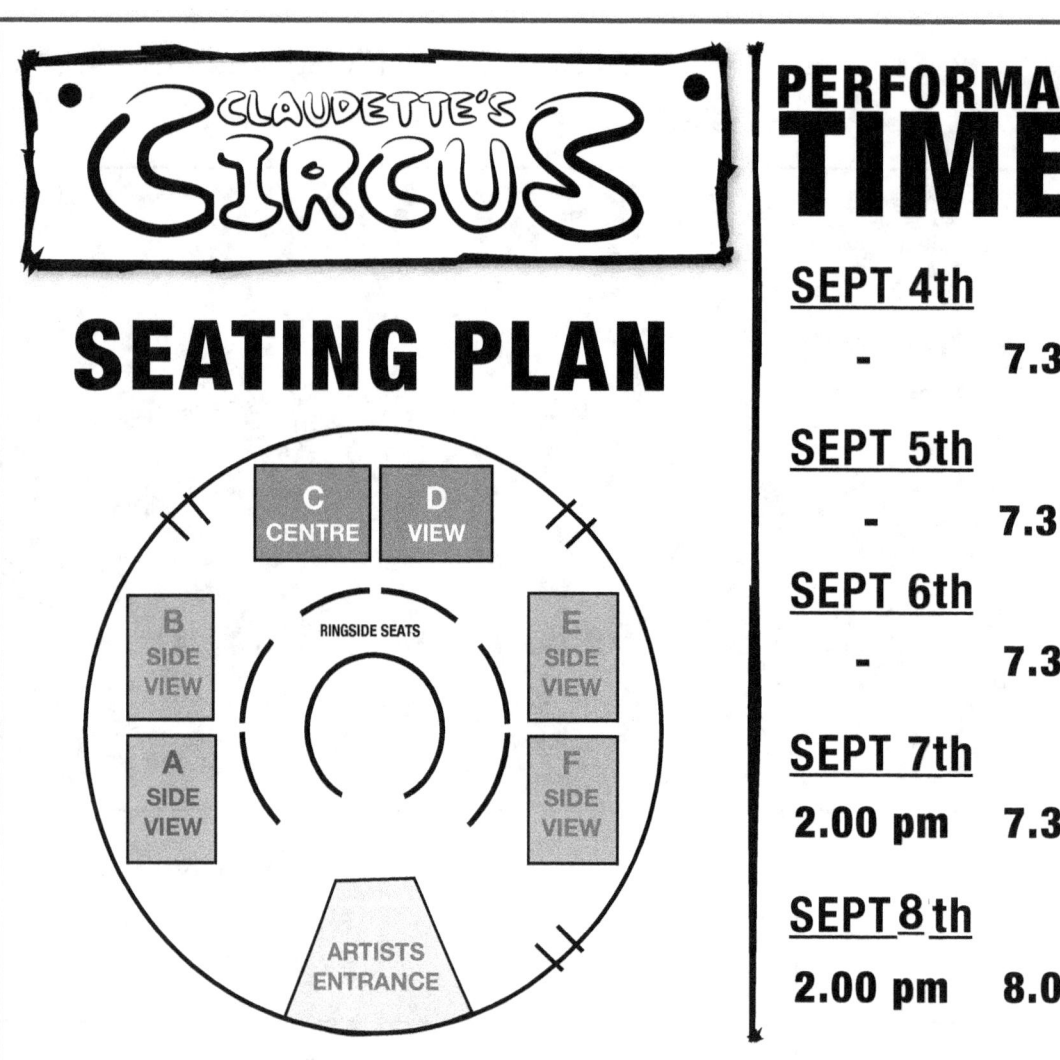

TYPE OF SEAT	ADULTS	CHILDREN (2-14 YEARS)	PEOPLE OVER 65
FRONT ROW (RINGSIDE)	£15	£10	£10
ROWS 2-3 (RINGSIDE)	£12	£8	£8
GRAND STAND: CENTRE VIEW	£8	£6	£6
GRAND STAND: SIDE VIEW	£6	£4	£4

Brainstorm the circus. Make a mind map.

These pages help you put your thoughts in a good order. Add your own ideas.

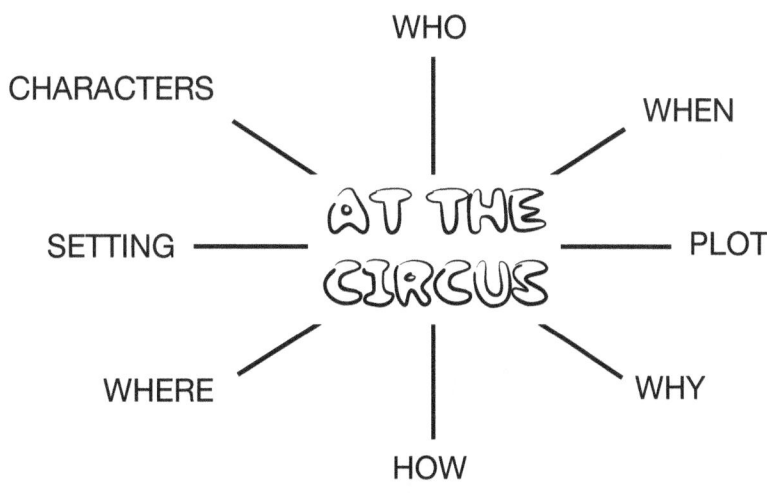

- an old walled town
- bright sky
- warm night

→

- big top (the main circus tent) set up in the car park.
- is brightly coloured with red and white stripes
- caravans/trailers spill onto pavement
- clutter narrow streets

↓

- band plays loudly
- echoing into the surrounding streets

←

- feeling of excitement

↓

- people queue to buy tickets
- enter big top to find seats

→

- eat pop corn and ice cream

↓

- delicious smell of hot dogs and burgers

Now jot down some ideas under these headings.

CLOWNS:

have bright red lips and a red nose

ride round on a tricycle

wear baggy trousers

make the audience boo or cheer

smash custard pies in peoples' faces

throw buckets of water

laugh hysterically
cry loudly

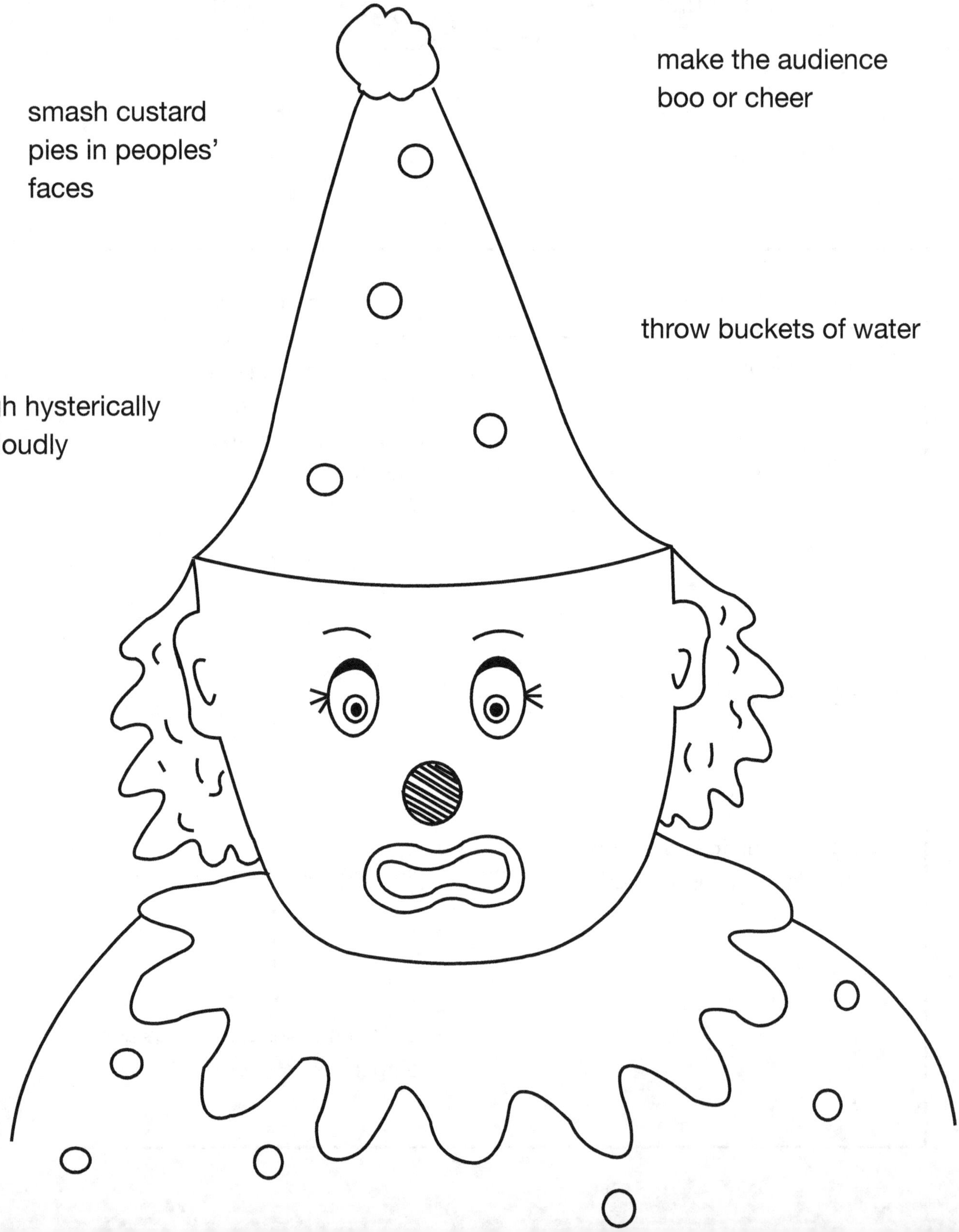

RINGMASTER:

- enters ring
- wears red top hat and tails
- rides round on his horse
- introduces acts to audience

JUGGLERS:

- throw balls up in the air and catch them
- spin plates on sticks
- juggle batons of fire

ELEPHANTS:

- wear head-dresses
- swing their trunks
- kick a ball

LIONS:

- run in
- leap through hoops
- sit on their stands
- obey their trainer

TIGER:

- walks round on his lead

THE BARE BACK RIDERS:

- ride white horses
- wear head-dresses with feathers
- wear fantastic plumes on their heads
- gallop round the ring
- stand up on their horses' backs and balance.
- perform daring stunts

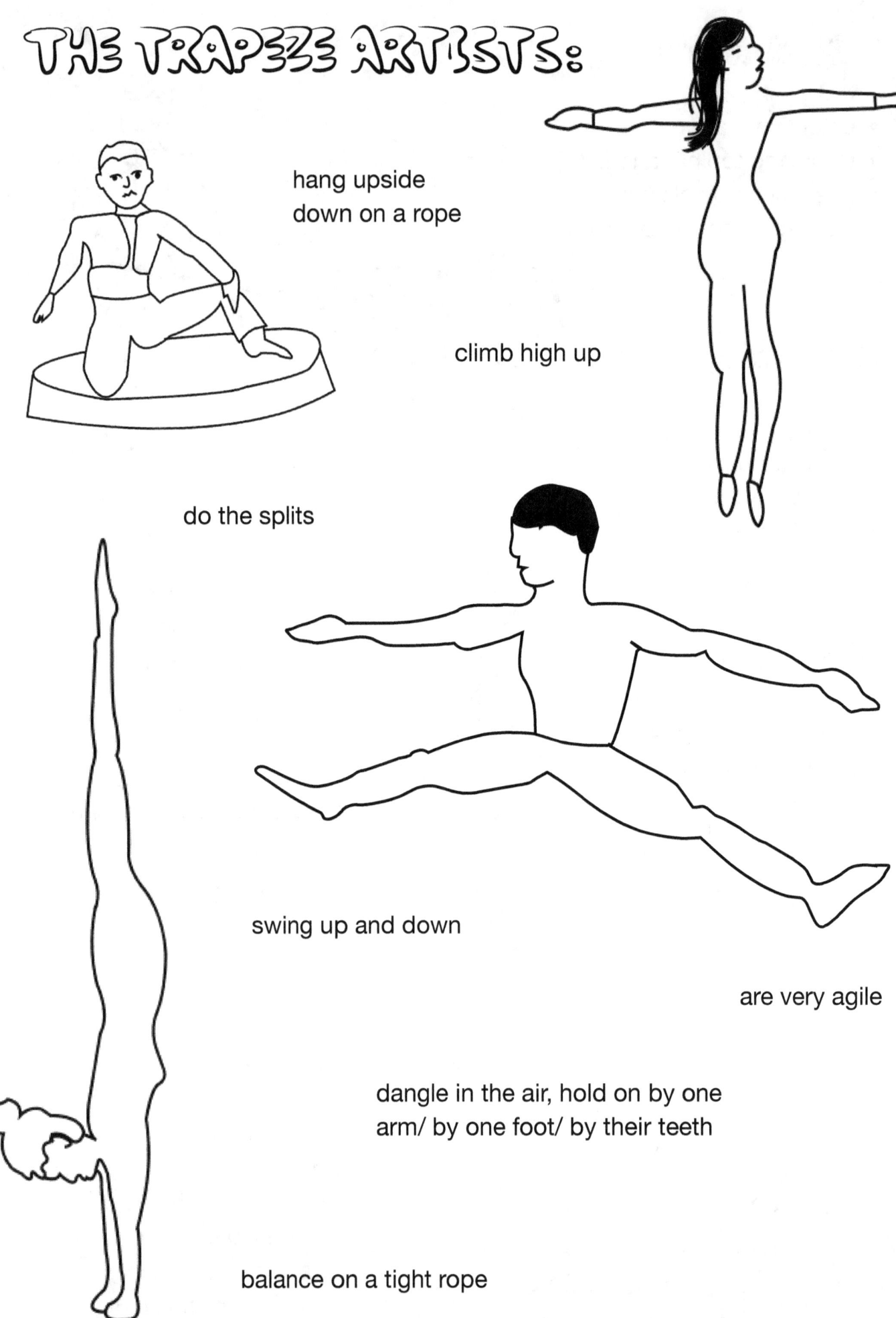

FIFTEEN MINUTE INTERVAL:

You can buy:

- ice cream
- popcorn
- sweets
- a souvenir from the circus shop

AUDIENCE:

- applauds
- cheers
- claps

THE ACROBATS:

- perform energetic dance routines
- perform daring stunts with fire and knives
- skip with ropes
- form human pyramids

WHEN THE PERFORMANCE WINDS UP:

- audience are clapping
- the lights go on
- people get up from their seats and queue to get out
- people chatter excitedly
- people discuss the show
- people look happy

Can we make this into a story?

Let's write fiction.

Read the plan below and then turn over.

Setting	• The circus comes to a small French seaside town.
Character	• You go with Mum, Dad, brother and sister.
Start of Plot	• You buy a ticket and enter the big top to find your seat. You smell the sawdust in the circus ring and feel the excitement.
Develop the action	• The lights dim and the show starts. • The ringmaster introduces the acts. • There are: clowns, trapeze artists, animal acts, bare back riders, jugglers.
Introduce a complication	• There is a problem. • Something happens and it triggers off a whole chain of unexpected events.
Build up suspense	• What could happen?
Solve the problem with a resolution	• How is the problem solved? • How do the audience react? • What do they do? • Do they gasp? Do they cry out? • Do they cheer and clap? • When the show ends and the lights go on what do people say? • Do they discuss the show? • Are they happy?

Finish the circus story.   *The story is written in the PAST TENSE as if it happened yesterday.*

Continue the story from the second paragraph. In your writing, introduce a complication and build up tension.

The circus had arrived in the market square and there was a buzz in the old walled town. The band played loudly. Amber and her family were making their way towards the circus tent, walking round the caravans and lorries that spilled over the pavement. She felt excited. In fact, she felt so excited... she had butterflies in her stomach because she had never been to a circus before.

As they entered the big top, Amber peered through the dim light. There, she saw a crowd of people already seated round the ring, talking excitedly. The tent smelled strange - of sawdust. They took their seats. After a while the ringmaster opened the show, "It is with great pleasure I welcome you to Claudette's Circus."

Here are some ideas to help you...

- Two clowns rolled on to the stage, their faces painted white with bright red lips. One clown played the piano, but the other didn't like the noise so he slammed down the lid. The other clown got a bucket and... *(Is there a fight?)*
- To start with... the trapeze artist climbed a rope ladder to the top of the tent. She did some somersaults in the air. She held on with one hand... then by her leg... until Amber hardly dared to look. Then... *(Does she fall into the safety net?)*
- The bareback riders galloped round in sparkling leotards with feathers in their hair. They stood up on their horses on one leg... then they balanced on each others' shoulders... *(Does the act go wrong?)*
- The jugglers threw their batons high in the air and caught them skillfully, but then... *(Do they drop their batons?)*
- Then the lions raced in, leaping through their hoops proudly. They fixed their eyes on their trainer and obeyed each instruction, but suddenly... *(Does a lion escape?)*

Some people **disagree** with animals being in the circus. Here are some points they make:

- Animals are confined in small cages.
- They might be chained up for several hours a day.
- In travelling circuses, they spend hours in lorries being transported from place to place.
- Their trainers are mean because they make them work too hard practising their tricks.
- They are made to do things they don't want to do so humans can be entertained.

Other people **agree** with animals being in circuses. Here are some points they make:

- There is no scientific evidence to show that animals are harmed by being in the circus.
- They don't suffer stress because they are used to the circus way of life.
- They are well kept and get on well with their trainers.

What do you think? Do you agree or disagree? Write down your thoughts.

In my opinion ....
....
....
....
....
....

Have **FUN** with *poems*.

Clowns

In the circus are

Really funny, when they throw

Custard pies, or land

Upside down or

Slip and slide on a banana.

Every

Little

Elephant

Performs

Happily

At

Night

Time shows.

> Try making up an **acrostic poem** like these.

Recount a visit to the circus in three paragraphs.

- Have you ever been to the circus?
- Where did you go?
- When did you go to the circus?
- Which circus did you go to?
- Who did you go with?
- What did you like about:
    - the tent
    - the seats
    - the saw dust?
- Which performers did you enjoy watching?
- Which performers did you not enjoy watching? Why?
- If you could do some performing skills which ones would you choose?
- Why?

Make a **programme** for the show.

Claudette's Circus

List of performers:

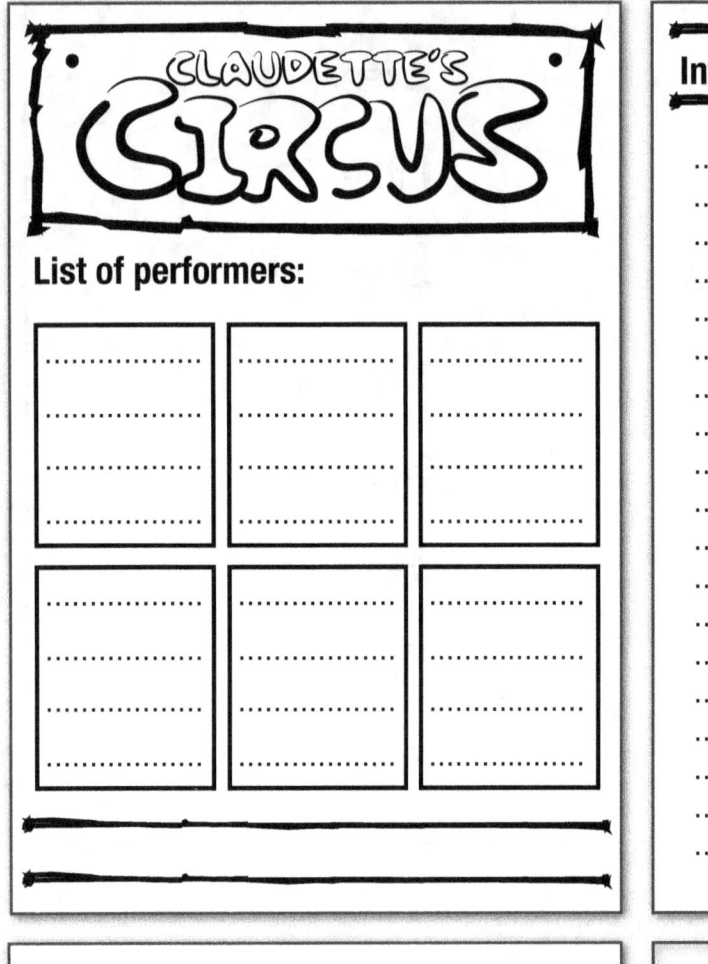

Information about the circus:

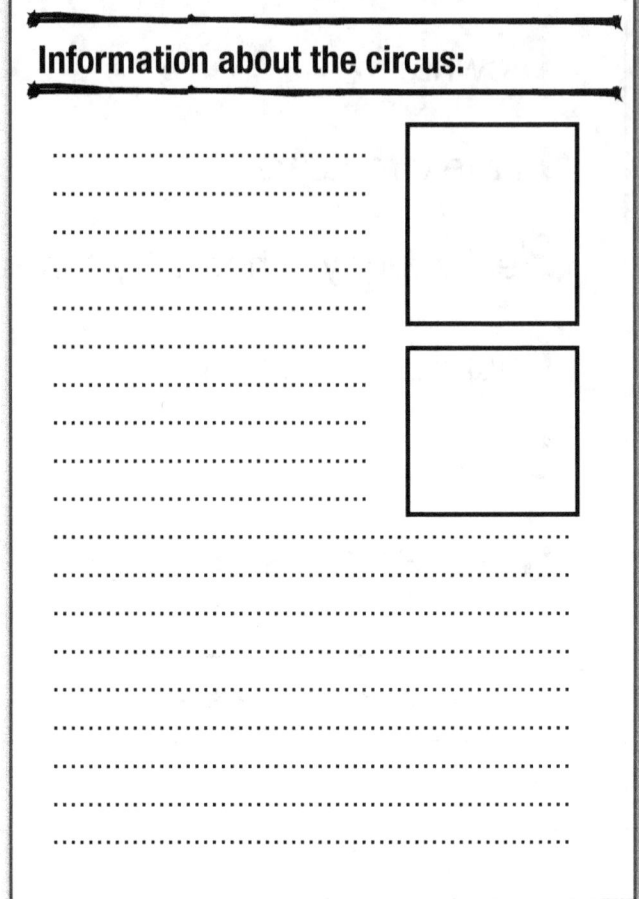

List of Acts in Order:

- Ring master introduces the ....
- ....
- Amazing Amy the elephant ....
- ....
- ....
- ....
- ....
- ....
- ....

The ringmaster says,

"Good afternoon ladies and gentleman. May I introduce you to Amazing Amy the ELEPHANT, she is ...."

REVIEWS of the SHOW

Write what people think....

"I enjoyed the show because ....
....
....
....
.........................."

"I didn't enjoy the show because..........
....
....
....
....
....
.........................."

Listen Live

Hi, I'm your D.J George...

... and I'm Christabelle.

How are you today, George?

I feel great. I'm really excited about the show tomorrow.

Me too!

I can't wait to be broadcasting live at the Fun Day on the beach.

It's going to be such fun. I've already packed my bikini. How about you?

I'll definitely be braving the waves. I've got my swimming shorts and my surfboard ready.

You listeners out there... don't forget to tune in tomorrow at 10 am for our road show. It will be a live broadcast from the beach, South Sands. Even better, if you can come down here and hear us live, we'd just love to see you wouldn't we Christabelle...

Yes, we want you all to be there in your thousands.

And bring lots of cash because there's going to be loads of stalls. There's donkey rides for the kids, sphere balls, bouncy castles, pitch and putt... and for those of you who are brave - trampolining, kite surfing, wake-boarding, power boat rides and loads more.

We're organising lots of competitions here at Guinea Pig FM Radio Station. There'll be stickers and holiday fun packs given away and loads of fab prizes up for grabs.

What fun competitions could they do?

- sumo wrestling
- ....
- ....

> This radio script is informal. It is written the way a radio presenter would talk, with shortened words and casual slang.

Then we've got a real treat for you. We've got an amazing line up of groups including ....

Who would you like to see?

- ....
- ....
- ....

At eight o'clock we've got Glitzy Mitzy performing live on the main stage.

Wow - she'll be amazing!

It's all being transmitted live for our viewers on Guine Pig FM, if you can't get down to South Sands.

But we want you all to come down.

Remember, all you listeners out there, this event is for charity. It is to raise money for this months cause - Beach Rescue.

It's really important that you support us. Just think what it would be like if you floated out to sea on your inflatable dinghy and you couldn't get back to shore. You were drifting out at sea getting further and further from the beach!

Those Beach Rescue guys would be with you in two minutes to bring you back to shore.

So we must raise enough money to support them. We need to exceed last years total that was a staggering 250 thousand pounds.

This year we can do even better.

Anyway, I thought we'd get the listeners to phone in with their rescue stories tonight. Text, e-mail or phone... just get them coming in.

We'll start reading them out after...
the next track...

What pop/rock music would you like to hear?

- ....

"We have Fin on the line."

"What have you got for us Fin?"

"I want to tell you about the day I got trapped."

"That sounds exciting..."

"My friend and I hired a holiday apartment on the rugged coast of North Devon – the views were spectacular there. On my first morning I couldn't wait to get down on the beach to explore. I started to walk along the beach towards the estuary where the river meets the sea. The pale yellow sand stretched ahead of me for miles. On one side of me, huge powerful waves swept onto the shore, making a rhythmic music, while on the other side, the dark, rocky cliff towered over me. I was as happy as a lark, as I walked with the warm sun on my face, listening to music on my i-pod and sucking mints. Little did I know, though - that Jon was looking out of the apartment window with horror, as he watched a lone figure disappearing into the distance. He had been to the area before. He knew the dangers. He knew you could be swept away by the incoming tide in seconds because the currents are strong. But I didn't know that; I didn't see the red flag flying – so I just kept walking without a care in the world."

"Oh no! That's so dangerous! What happened next?"

"It was not long after this that I turned round to look back. Then I saw the sun had disappeared and the sky was filled with ominous black clouds, that were approaching me rapidly. Soon, it started to pour down with rain. It was a huge torrent of rain with hailstones that stung my skin, so I looked for a place to shelter, under a ledge in the cliff. That's when I realised the sea was coming in. It was advancing on me at such a fast pace that the beach was disappearing. I looked from side to side, but there was nowhere to go – except up the big, sheer rock face. As there was no path, it would have been too dangerous to climb the cliffs without a safety harness or climbing equipment. This was scary because there was nowhere to escape to. Panic seized me."

"I'm not surprised. I would have been terrified. What did you do?"

"I squeezed my body into a narrow crevice and clung on to the prickly stem of a straggly plant that was growing out of the rock. The breakers (waves) began to crash onto the rocks around me. I stared down into the swirling, frothy water. My mind raced. It was too rough to swim and if I shouted for help, only the squawking sea gulls, circling over my head, would hear me cry. I was shaking. I was in shock! Would I drown?

There I stayed for three hours or more, listening to the same tune on my i-pod, with no supplies of food. I began to feel cold, weak and hungry, but I was scared to go to sleep in case I slipped to my death in the dark, deep and dismal water. I remember that feeling of despair in the bottom of my heart. It was awful, not knowing if I would live to tell the tale. I didn't even remember Jon back at the apartment, but he remembered me. He was beside himself with fear and anxiety and he had already reported me missing to the coast guard. They called up the Beach Rescue team. Little did I know as I gave in to thoughts of hopelessness, that the engines of the helicopter had already started up and it was hovering over the sea searching for me! Then, I heard the throbbing of an engine above me. I summoned all my strength to wave frantically, but they didn't see me. I waved, screamed and hollowed, as they circled a second time. Then I saw a man descending on a rope. It was the best moment of my life so far. He hoisted me up into the safety of the helicopter where Jon was sitting. That's when I vowed I would always be sensible in future. I would read information, look out for signs and make sure I was properly equipped."

"Wow, what a story. Now, we have Nadia on the line."

"I was on holiday with my cousin at the sea side. That morning, we had been exploring the rock pools with our nets, while auntie and uncle did some shopping. We had collected a whole bucket of little creatures - shrimps, tiny fish and crabs... Then it was time to go back for lunch. It seemed a long way round the official path, which zig-zagged across the cliff and it looked quicker to climb straight up the steep incline. We thought we'd give it a go - even though Dan's parents had given us strict instructions not to climb the cliffs because they were crumbling.

At first it was quite easy to clamber up the cliff face and we felt like real mountaineers. We lodged our feet on the stones, like rungs in a ladder. We clutched at the straggly shrubs growing out of the rock face. Somehow we heaved ourselves up the steep slope. Then, the cliff got even steeper. We were out of breath and our progress slowed down. A whole hour passed and we were still only half way up. Then, I put my foot forward and dislodged a whole pile of stones. They started to hurtle down as the cliff began to crumble away. This made me lose my grip, and as my cousin watched me, I started to slip down the cliff with a pile of rubble, gathering speed, going faster and faster. At that moment my whole life seemed to flash before me. Would I survive? Suddenly, I hit a gnarled old tree that was growing out of the ledge. It stopped my fall, but as I looked down down, I saw I was perched on a narrow ravine. My ankle throbbed. Could it be broken? I lay there too weak to shout 'help'! Meanwhile my cousin was half way up the cliff, but he realised it was too dangerous to climb to the top. He tried phoning his mum on his mobile, but there was no signal. He had no choice, but to scramble... very slowly... down... backwards, terrified that he would cause another landslide. He said he felt sick as a dog because he was so scared and he didn't know what had happened to me.

Finally, he descended to the beach and alerted the Beach Rescue. They searched the cliff for me immediately. Some rescuers arrived with proper climbing equipment. A woman clambered down on a rope with a helmet on. She strapped me onto a stretcher and another man hoisted me up the cliff. It would have been exciting if it hadn't been me! Then, I was put in an ambulance at the top of the cliff. I remember seeing my cousin's pale face. At that point I decided that I would always obey instructions and never ignore advice again - especially when it comes to cliffs...!"

My dad took the wrong route on holiday. He took a mountain road and it was treacherous. It was winding up a very tall mountain and looking down was making me dizzy. There was a big drop and it was getting dark. We didn't know whether to continue driving or camp by the roadside.

Write the story.

"Katy has texted in"

I went on a roller coaster. We were just circling for the second time and I could see amazing views from the top... and then we stopped. I was terrified because I'm not even that keen on heights. I thought - will I be rescued and have to climb down? But my friend was loving it. She thought it was great and sat back in her seat to relax!

Write the story.

My friend and I saw a power boat sign advertising a trip out to sea. We paid our money and the boat set out. It hurtled through the water, jumping through the waves at great speed. It was thrilling. Then it turned round to go back, but it stopped... Oh no, the engine had failed! We were stuck in a small powerboat out to sea.

Write the story.

Let's *practise* writing **FICTION**

I am writing a story.

I am thinking of a character and what he or she looks like:
- eyes
- hair
- face
- height

→

I am thinking what his or her personality is like:
- happy
- sad
- naughty
- good
- polite
- courteous
- sensible
- loud
- noisy
- funny

I am thinking:
- how he or she behaves
- how he or she feels
- how he or she speaks
- what he or she likes to do

→

I am wondering what other people think of him.

I am thinking that my character:
- frowns — angrily
- mumbles — quietly
- sings — tunefully
- chuckles — gleefully
- whispers — softly
- listens — quietly
- smiles — happily

I am matching the verbs with the adverbs.

→

I am thinking of a setting.

I am writing some details to describe the setting.

- ....
- ....
- ....
- ....
- ....
- ....
- ....

I am jotting down the key points. - .... - .... - .... - .... - .... →	I am thinking what I can: - see - hear - taste - touch - smell
I am thinking about the atmosphere of my setting. →	I am saying: - Where is it? - What is there? - What is the weather like? - What people are there? - What do you do there? - What do I think of it?
I want to create atmosphere by using good nouns and adjectives: - amazing views - rugged coast - pale yellow sand - huge powerful waves - ominous dark clouds →	I am thinking of a plot.
I am thinking: - What are my characters doing? - What happens in my story to trigger off some actions or problems. →	I am deciding how I can build up suspense and an excellent climax, so my readers are on the edge of their seat.

I am deciding how my story is wound up, resolved or ended; using a happy, sad, cliffhanger or moral ending. → **I am organising my work.**

I am starting a new paragraph for:
- a new event
- a new place
- a new time

or in non-fiction
- a new point of view.

→ I am using connectives to start a new paragraph to link ideas.
- but
- yet
- so
- moreover
- also
- furthermore
- what is more
- for instance
- for example
- such as
- however
- therefore

I am using a <u>topic sentence</u> at the beginning of a new paragraph, which contains the main point of the paragraph. The rest of the paragraph will explain the topic sentence. ←

Mrs Barker's class write stories.

They can choose from different genres or types of story.

Writers use these techniques. In their stories they:

- have an interesting opening to make the reader want to read on.

- have an ending that the reader will remember (a happy ending, a sad ending, a cliff hanger or a moral ending).

- use flash backs.

- use dialogue to move the story on, show what the characters are doing and how they relate to each other.

- use interesting nouns, adjectives, good verbs and adverbs. Use similes - 'as bold as a lion' and metaphors - 'You're an angel.'

- write in first person (I) or third person (he or she) (as a fly on the wall).

- write directly to the reader.

Read this rescue story and then write your own version.

- Introduce the character setting and plot in paragraph 1.

> The snow in the mountains was melting. It had been a very warm winter. "Looks like the river might overflow," warned Uncle Toby. His words drifted on the wind as Ellie shut the door. "I'm just going down to the village, Uncle," she shouted, heading in the direction of her pony Mitizi's field. Nothing would separate Ellie from her beloved pony. They went everywhere together. If she needed to get some provisions for Uncle, she would ride him down the track to the edge of the village and tether him to a post. She would say, "Wait here little one" stroking his mane and in reply, he would nuzzle his soft nose against her.

- Develop the plot with actions and complications in paragraph 2.

> On this day, Ellie went over to the shed to get Mitzi but he wasn't there. "He must have wandered out of the gate," she thought to herself. She searched the path but he was nowhere to be seen. Then, she crossed the rickety, old bridge; it seemed to be swaying more than usual. She leaned over the side of the bridge; the water in the river was higher and it was flowing swiftly. Ellie froze! Her heart began to race because she saw something struggling in the river. "Hold on my beauty," she gasped "I am coming." In reply came a weak neigh. Ellie slithered down the bank to the water's edge where she found her little pony stuck in the mud...

- Build up suspense. Use words like suddenly, Help! Help!, screamed, yelled and gasped. Plus, use short sentences and repetition. Use punctuation - ... ! ?

> Ellie screamed, "Kick, kick as hard as you can." She seized his tail, she tugged at it. "Help! Help!" she yelled but there was no one around. The pony struggled to free himself from the mud but he was stuck fast. The gushing, swirling river was rising rapidly. Would he drown? Fear seized her whole body. She was petrified *(terrified, shaking, shivering)*. Tears streamed down her face but she would not let go.

- <u>Reach a climax</u>. Make the ending interesting. This is a happy ending.

> As Ellie struggled to pull her pony out of the murky water, the river continued to rise. Every time she thought her pony was coming out, he slipped back into the swirling water but she was determined to hang on. At that moment there was a horrible creaking sound as the angry water washed away part of the bridge. In one desperate effort, the pony managed to kick himself free from the mud, push his hooves into the firm reeds of the bank and heave his great body out of the raging water. "Oh thank goodness you are safe," she whispered, hugging him and stroking his soft ears. In return, he licked her hand. After this, they hurried along the path to the village dripping wet and covered in mud. Ellie was able to warn everyone she met of the dangerous bridge and when she arrived in the village she contacted the police who closed the road. Ellie was a heroine. She had rescued Mitzi and saved the lives of many others.

Read this rescue story and then write your own version.

Grant and his friends, Toni and Matt, were slowly plodding up the icy mountain path to see the stunning view at the top... but they did not get that far. The deep snow, which had fallen overnight, had covered everything in its reach in white powder and made the track excessively slippery. The DJ (on local radio) had reported that the snow lay two metres deep on the slopes. It glistened in the morning sunlight. The young people, who were on a new year break, were wrapped up warm in their padded jackets to protect themselves from the freezing temperatures. Their cheeks were burning in the cold, their eyes were stinging from the glare of the white snow. Despite all this, they were determined to make the most of their time here.

It was not long before they came to a log cabin, where they stopped to catch their breath. Outside, there was an old handwritten sign. Grant translated it into English. "Skis for hire. Great deals on offer." The guy in charge eyed them up shiftily, "You don't need any experience on the beginner slopes," he growled in broken English. Grant hadn't learnt to ski but it didn't look difficult so he handed over the money. To their relief the ski lift was working. On their arrival at the beginner's slope, they put on their skis. The snow was deeper than they expected. It was rather steep. Had they come too far? They were slithering, sliding and slipping.
"It's easy," boasted Grant, as he skimmed across the icy snow and began to descend rapidly down the icy slope, getting faster and faster. "Look I can do it," he bragged to his friends. "I don't need lessons." In an instant, he lost his balance, he skidded, he somersaulted, he turned over three times and he landed in the snow with a · Bump, Bump, Bump!

Toni and Matt were shocked. They didn't know what to do as they looked down at him laying pale and helpless in the snow. "Can you get up?" a passing skier panted. "Do you need help?"
"My shoulder hurts," muttered Grant.
"I'll get the mountain rescue team out," she murmured, dialing them up on her mobile. They arrived shortly and lifted Grant onto the snow mobile and took him back to the ski resort, where he was airlifted to the nearest hospital by helicopter. (Sadly he couldn't appreciate the view.) The doctors gave him a full examination but his shoulder was only badly bruised. Later, Grant returned to the hotel where his anxious friends were waiting for him. What do you think he said? "I've booked up some ski lessons for next weekend," he beamed. "Who's up for it?"

Read this ghost story and then write one of your own in the first person.

When I opened that clue, I was overcome with such fearful feelings that prickly shivers ran up and down my spine. It read, 'Lift the latch of the old black barn and go in. You will find the last clue hidden in there.' We were on a discovery holiday at an old farm house. It was a Tuesday evening after supper and Jon, our leader, had organised a surprise treasure hunt.

"Im not going in there," I insisted firmly to the others in my group.

"Why not! Don't be such a wimp."

"Things happen in there," I persisted. "People have seen things. Horrible things! There are awful screams heard there at night," I whimpered softly. I dug my heels in and refused to budge, but my friends forced me to go with them. They dragged me over and before I knew it, we were pulling open the old creaky door. It groaned ominously as it swung open and shut with a bang.

Inside the barn, it was quite oppressive (airless), It was stifling, it was stuffy and the pungent smell of dried hay was overpowering. Was it my imagination or was there a sinister feeling about the place? It was so dingy, so dark, but for the chinks of light that crept quietly through the gaps of wood. As my eyes readjusted to the dimness, I could pick out forbidding forms; old bits of farm machinery, old wheels that hadn't been used for years and whose shapes were casting monstrous shadows across the floor. We started to search for the clue, our fingers feeling frantically into every nook and cranny. It was then I heard something in the rafters above me. There was a rustling, shuffling and shaking sound. 'Was there something up there?' I asked myself... My heart started to beat faster. It was true. It was the phantom of the barn. At that moment, there was a horrible (ominous) screech. It was there. I saw it there. It was white and it had a huge face and piercing eyes and it flew straight down towards me, beating its wings.

"Help!" I screamed. "It's the ghost. Run!"

At that moment, I moved rapidly. I flung open the barn door and legged it into the cool night air. Everyone in my group raced after me like frightened sheep, hollering their heads off. We all headed down the path at lightning speed; a line of shrieking children. Faster and faster we ran, united by one thought: to distance ourselves from that black barn. As we turned the corner, I saw a horrified Jon, our leader, approaching us. "Stop running!" he ordered. Taken by surprise, I lost my footing and fell with a bump on the path. When I sat up, the children in my team were standing around me, all huffing and puffing. John was looking at my knee.

"It really hurts," I whispered.

"You'll be fine. It's not badly hurt." Everyone was asking the same question. Why are you being such a drama queen? What did you see? Why did you run like that?

"A horrible ghost flew at me beating its wings," I answered.

"More like a mother owl protecting her nest of babies from you lot," laughed Jon. I was not so sure he was right. What do you think?

Make a page of difficult words. Use a thesaurus to find words that mean the same - synonyms. Here are a few to start you off.

Discover	find out, learn, spot, reveal, recognise
Organise	arrange, run, plan, set up, prepare
Search	check, explore, probe, investigate, hunt, seek, look for, hunt for, pursue
Eerie	uncanny, strange, frightening, ghostly, weird, mysterious, scary, sinister, unearthly, supernatural
Monstrous	shocking, huge, great, vast, enormous, immense, gigantic, colossal, tremendous
Horrible	awful, terrible, terrifying, grim, fearful, shocking, dreadful, appalling
Scream	cry, yell, shriek, bellow, screech, howl, shout, bawl, squeal, yelp
Fling	throw, toss, chuck
Creaked	squeak, grind, scrape, groan, grate, screech, scratch
Ominous	threatening, menacing, sinister, dark, foreboding, grim, fateful
Tripped	fall, stumble, topple, lose your footing
Whispered	murmur, mutter, mumble, speak in a hushed tone, say softly

A realistic story with a flashback. Read this story then write one of your own.

Lilly writes about her brother when he was a small child.

At the age of four my little brother had the reputation of being a dare devil. In the playground, he would climb to the top of the climbing frame and hang upside down, before recklessly zooming down the slide at great speed. He would swing so high on the tyre that he nearly did a flip over. His agility on the rope ladder beat that of any monkey. Mum said that it was a good job the council had put down a safety surface to land on if he fell. Despite his boldness, he had one weakness. There was one thing that sent him shouting, shrieking and screaming. Dogs!

It was small dogs that freaked him out (terrified him). You know the kind: long floppy ears, bodies like sausages, big sad eyes and a wagging tail. I remember we passed a dog just like this. Ben, as he was called, had just been let off his lead in the park, by his owner, Liz. He was busy exploring his surroundings, sniffing here and there, when he picked up the scent of some yummy food - crisps - smoky bacon flavoured crisps, wafting through the air. He followed the smell until he came to my brother sitting on a bench eating a packet of crisps. Of course, the dog jumped up boisterously, his tongue lolling out for a taste.
"Go away," yelled my brother crossly, backing away, but the dog carried on rubbing him with his wet nose. Now my brother panicked. Overcome with terror, he ran fast. He sprinted across the park. The dog, thinking it was a good game, chased him. My brother increased his pace and the dog, in high spirits, bolted after him, his jaws wide open.
"Help me!" cried my brother.
"Come back Ben," cried the distraught Liz. "He won't hurt you."
"Eeek, Eeek," he screamed.

My brother didn't hear a word. He ran wildly on until he disappeared into the distance, with the dog hot on his heels. I must confess I was splitting my sides with laughter. Worse than this, he didn't see the bin until he went 'smack' right into it. Then he fell flat on his face amongst the rubbish. He made such a song and dance (threw such a tantrum), that the poor dog didn't know what to do. He just stopped dead... and stared dumfounded. What was this monster in front of him? It had an old soggy box on its head. Disappointed that the fun was over, the dog quietly trotted back to his owner with his ears hung low... while my brother gradually untangled himself from the contents of the bin, looking red faced and slightly embarrassed, as he returned to me. Sometimes I still tease my brother about the day he fell into the rubbish bin. It also explains why my brave brother (that plucky, rash and reckless boy) is still scared of dogs.

A flashback goes back in time and gives some information about a character in the plot.

Read this modern version of a traditional story and then write one of your own.

1, 2, 3, Wishes

Once upon a time there were a brother and sister called Sophie and Jon. They lived in a ramshackled old cottage, with no curtains at the window, paint peeling off the door and a broken down T.V. set, which they couldn't afford to repair. One day the girl was sitting sadly in front of the blank T.V. screen, wishing she could turn it on to watch cartoons. Her brother was reading a book called 'The Magic Lamp.' All of a sudden there was a loud clatter and an old rusty lamp landed at her feet. She was surprised, to say the least, but being an inquisitive child she picked it up. As she was sometimes disagreeable by nature, she thought, "Oh no what am I meant to do with this." She tried rubbing it gently and to her amazement a genie appeared saying, "I'm at your command, you have three wishes." For once Sophie was completely speechless and just stared. "Tell me your three wishes," the genie repeated impatiently.

A moment later, the girl stammered "You can see what I want. It is a new 3D wide screen T.V. and a D.V.D player as well,"
"Your wishes have been granted," replied the genie. "And your last wish, what is that going to be?"
"I'm not sure," answered the girl as she fumbled with the switches on her new T.V.
"I'll come back later to grant your third wish," continued the genie. "In the mean time allow me to take something in return for my precious lamp."
"Go ahead," responded the girl thoughtlessly. The genie beckoned to Jon, "Come with me," he whispered and they both disappeared in a puff of smoke. When the programme, she was watching, finished, the girl started to think about her third wish.
"Jon, do you think we should have a... computer?" He didn't reply. "Jon, Jon," she called out frantically, but he was nowhere to be seen. She ran from room to room. Her heart was beating fast... "Jon answer me."

At that moment, she remembered the genie's words. "I'll have to take something in exchange for the lamp." Now she was convinced that he had taken her brother. In desperation she started to rub the lamp madly. The genie appeared in front of her.
"Genie, my third wish is to give me my brother back now."
" Ok, your final wish is granted," grunted the genie, "but first you must hand me back my lamp." Sophie clung to the lamp defiantly. She was determined to keep it. She was not going to be ordered about by anyone, not even a genie. She, Sophie, would take control of the lamp, so she rubbed it a second time, commanding,
"Lamp, give me my brother back in exchange for the genie. There was another puff of smoke, followed by a big bang and the genie was replaced by Jon. She hugged him tightly and words poured out of his mouth, as he spoke of his adventure. But Sophie wasn't listening. She was investigating her new lamp. It must be valuable she thought, and it was. The children never wanted for anything ever again.

Read the first two paragraphs of this mystery story and then write an exciting ending.

There was a loud rumbling sound like thunder and to my horror the rocky entrance of the passage shut tightly. I clawed at the face of the solid brick wall, but there was no crack. The door had closed on me and I was trapped. My eyes adjusted to the weird grey light. I saw that I was in a deep underground passage that stretched before me. I had no alternative, but to go on.

Down the dark passage I stepped, moving forward cautiously because it was slippery underfoot. I groped my way along the narrow tunnel. It was getting so tight that I had to tread sideways and grasp the slimy seaweed that covered the wall. Then the passage became so low that I had to crouch on my hands and knees. I followed the mysterious grey light, that led me to a cave and there it lighted the ground. It was then I spied a strange footstep, half human, half animal indented into the soft sand floor. I started to feel around the rocks and crevices in the cave to see if I could find any further clues that something had been there before me. Then I heard a low throaty growl, like something breathing nearby... Suddenly, a shiver went down my spine. Was I alone? I turned around and it was at that moment our eyes met...

....
....
....
....
....
....
....
....
....

When you write to describe, use the five senses - seeing, feeling, tasting, smelling. Use impressive vocabulary, similes and metaphors, alliteration. personification and onomatopoeia to conjure up atmosphere.

Read the realistic story and then write one of your own.

Kim remembers when she learnt to ride her big bike.
(She moves her story on with dialogue)

I complained to my mum,
"I still can't ride my big bike. You said you'd teach me but you're always busy."
"OK", said Mum. "We'll go down to the park this afternoon when I have finished the jobs."
The bike, which was my first proper bike, had been a present for my last birthday. It was bright and shiny without any scratches. I'd only ridden it up and down the road with Dad supporting the saddle to make sure I didn't fall. Secretly, I was a bit worried about riding it properly, because I didn't want to break it or spoil the shiny paint. More than this, I was terrified of falling off. I was useless at balancing and without Dad there... well, I'd just end up a heap on the floor.

"We're nearly at the park", exclaimed Mum, as she drove. I hope the bike is secure on the bike carrier. Soon, we arrived at the park and pulled into the car park.
"There's a space over there," I pointed out as mum swung into it. We unfixed the bike from its carrier and I put on my cycle helmet and mounted the saddle. Both feet on the ground, I straddled over to the grassy field where I was going to practise riding my bike.
"Off you go then," said Mum. "It's soft here so you won't hurt yourself if you fall." I put my feet on the peddles, cycled a short distance and stopped. Mum clapped.
"Try again," she encouraged. I managed to go on even further this time.
"Look at me now," I boasted, slamming on the brakes. "I can balance. I really am riding my bike. I can do it."
"Well done," Mum shouted. "Go faster." Soon I was hurtling along on my own. I was feeling so pleased with myself, but I didn't see the stone. "Oh no," I yelled. I applied the brakes. There was a sharp screeching sound. Suddenly, I was jolted; I was lurched forward. Then my bike folded up beneath me and it went clattering and crashing down. It lay sprawled in a ditch and I was catapulted into a nearby bed of nettles.
"Ahh," I moaned!

"Are you alright love?" said Mum, running up horrified. "Can you stand up?" I struggled up painfully.
"I hurt all over." I whimpered.
"Oh no! There's lumps and bumps all over your legs," she stammered. "A rash is coming up all over your arm. You've been stung badly by those stinging nettles."
"It hurts," I cried jumping up and down. "It itches, it stings, it's driving me mad."
"Let's get you back to the chemist and get something to put on it." Mum picked up what was left of my bike and bundled it into the car and we drove to the pharmacy. We saw Mum's friend Andrea, the pharmacist.
"You have been in the wars young lady, but I've got something that will fix it. It will be just fine." She gave me a cream to apply three times a day. I can't begin to tell you how soothing it was when I applied it to those bumps. Mum always says you can depend on Andrea to come up with the right potion. When Dad came home, the rash had completely gone. Now, I needed a miracle cure for my bike.
"What have you been up to today?" he asked. I announced proudly.
"I've been riding my bike. I'm really good now."
"That's great. Show me after dinner."
"Ok... but first my bike needs a small repair..." Dad gave me one of those looks. "Nothing much," I assured him.

Use different words to begin sentences.

I complained to my Mum...

Mum replied, "Ok, we'll..."

The bike has been...

It was...

Dad was teaching me to ride by...

Secretly, I was worried that...

and...

We arrived at the...

Mum unfixed the bike from...

I cycled a short distance and...

Then I rode even further saying...

After this, I...

but I didn't see...

My wheels swerved and I...

Then, my mum said, "..."

She noticed that I...

I replied, "I..."

We drove quickly to...

where I saw...

Andrea gave me... which...

Later, I'd forgotten...

because I told Dad...

Paragraph 1

introduction, character, setting and plot

- girl complains no one has taught her to ride her bike.
- Mum promises to take her to the park.
- girl afraid that she will fall off or damage her bike.

Paragraph 2

action, problem, complication, suspense, crisis

- arrive in park
- take bike off carrier
- girl mounts bike
- rides a little way and stops
- rides further and then hurtles along at great speed
- doesn't see stone
- crashes and falls into stinging nettles

Paragraph 3

resolution, ending

- Mum horrified
- sees nettle rash
- lots of bumps on girls arms and legs
- go straight to pharmacist
- get soothing cream
- forgets about injury
- tells Dad she can ride her bike

If we empathise with a character, we see things from his or her point of view. (It is like putting on someone's shoes so we know how they feel.)

Mrs Barker says, "If you could be somebody or something else, who would you be?" The children of her class write stories and she puts them on the wall.

Aaron writes:

I am an old man scarecrow now, with a torn overcoat and a floppy hat. I am worn out after years of standing out in the fields, but I wouldn't change my life for any ones. I am a good-natured fellow, with a good heart who you can depend on. I am never lonely because I am always surrounded by my friends – the bugs and small creatures that live in my field.

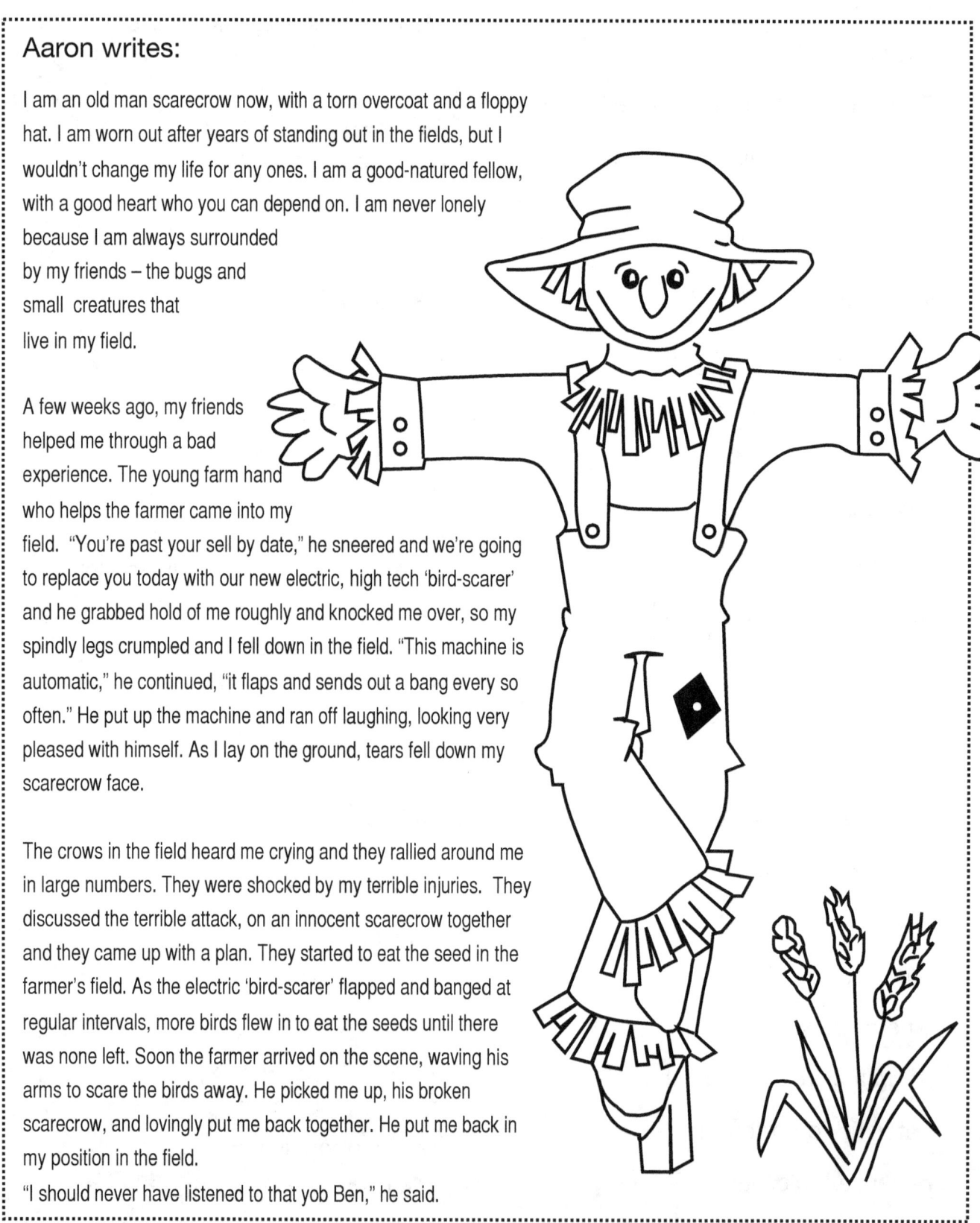

A few weeks ago, my friends helped me through a bad experience. The young farm hand who helps the farmer came into my field. "You're past your sell by date," he sneered and we're going to replace you today with our new electric, high tech 'bird-scarer' and he grabbed hold of me roughly and knocked me over, so my spindly legs crumpled and I fell down in the field. "This machine is automatic," he continued, "it flaps and sends out a bang every so often." He put up the machine and ran off laughing, looking very pleased with himself. As I lay on the ground, tears fell down my scarecrow face.

The crows in the field heard me crying and they rallied around me in large numbers. They were shocked by my terrible injuries. They discussed the terrible attack, on an innocent scarecrow together and they came up with a plan. They started to eat the seed in the farmer's field. As the electric 'bird-scarer' flapped and banged at regular intervals, more birds flew in to eat the seeds until there was none left. Soon the farmer arrived on the scene, waving his arms to scare the birds away. He picked me up, his broken scarecrow, and lovingly put me back together. He put me back in my position in the field.
"I should never have listened to that yob Ben," he said.

Now, write your own scarecrow story, as if you were the scarecrow.

Use different words and phrases to start sentences. Join ideas with connectives. You can use these examples to help you, but it is better to write your own version.

- I am an...

  with ... (*appearance*)

- In the field where I live, I am considered to be ... (*character*)

- My friends are...

- and ... (*setting*)

- Last week, I was doing my job scaring...

- Ben the young farm assistant put up an...

- He said it was more efficient because...

- Then he knocked me...

  so my...

- I felt so... that

- The crows in the field heard and they...

- They were filled with...

- After this, they ignored the electric bird scarer and...

- When the farmer arrived on the scene, he decided...

- He put me...

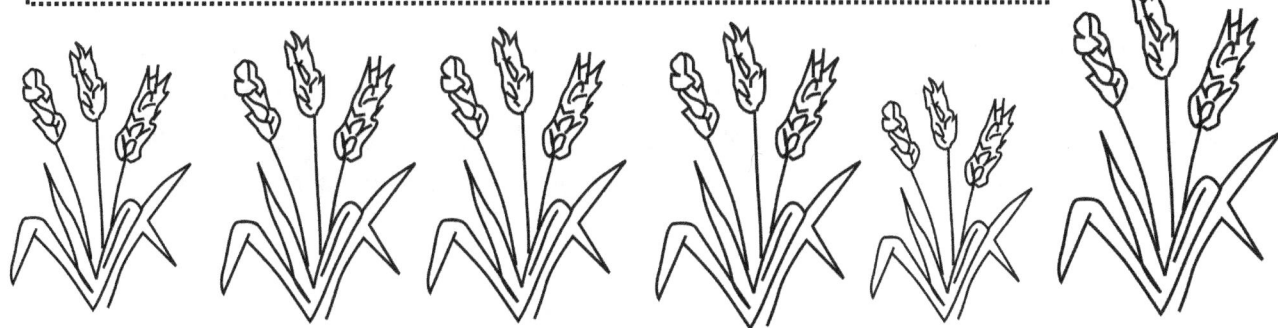

Pretend you are an object like an old car or a model. Write your own story.

Josh writes:

I was born in 2003 in a factory. As soon as the painter appeared with his spray gun, I knew I was going to be different from the other cars. I was painted a brilliant shade of purple. My first owner was a new driver named Matt. He had a young wife and a black and white dog called Sebastian. The three owners looked after me well and every weekend we would drive for miles in the country. As time went by, I didn't feel so well, because I was due for a service. There were aches and pains in my clutch and my brake pads were worn.

My family had been staying with friends in the country and they decided to drive home along the coastal road. The narrow road twisted and turned along the top of the cliff. It was starting to get dark and my dim headlights were finding it difficult to see in front of me. Suddenly, to my horror, I lost control. I started to career down a steep hill at great speed. The dog, Sebastian sensed the danger. The young wife cried out to her husband, "Please be careful." I was going faster and faster. I couldn't stop because my brakes had failed.
"Help! Help!" the driver screeched. "We're out of control." The wife screamed, the dog barked and I could feel sweat dripping down my windows. What was going to happen to us?

I didn't have time to think clearly, but I had to save my family. I had to act now. I saw my chance ahead. There was an open gate leading to a field on the right side of the road. I made a sharp turn into the bumpy track and raced through the gate. I started to drive through the thick mud in the field, terrifying a herd of cows. My troubles weren't over. We were being pursued by a big, black bull, which had been angered by the terrifying sight of a run away car in his field and was charging after us aggressively. Worse than this, the thick mud was clogging up my wheels and we were slowing down. Then we stopped altogether. Everyone scrambled out and started to run to safety. That is how I came to have a large dent in my shiny purple paintwork – where the bull had butted me furiously. However, later in the evening, I felt proud, when my owners returned with the break down truck and they told the technician that their little purple car had a mind if its own and it had saved them from great danger.

Now write the story as if you were an old car.

Use different words and phrases to start sentences. Join ideas with connectives. You can use these examples to help you, but it is better to write your own version.

- I was born in...

  and I am different from other cars because...

- My first owner was a young...

- Every weekend we...

- As time went by I felt ... because...

- My family had been staying with...

  and drove back along...

  which were...

- It was...

- Suddenly we came to a steep hill...

  and...

- The people and the dog started to scream, "... "

- I felt...

  because I was...

  so I made a ... into a ...

- Then we were...

- After a while, we stopped in...

  and my owners..

- The bull, scared of the runaway car, charged at me and made...

- Later, my owners came back...

- They said I had...   I felt...

Tilly writes:

From the depths of the loft I cried out, "Help! Help! Get me out of here. I demand to be let out right now." My previous owners had abandoned me years ago. They had packed me away in a box and left me in the loft to rot and to become a choky ball of dust. I had fallen into total disrepair. My paint was peeling, my wheels were stiff and I didn't know if my clockwork mechanism worked. I was squashed in by an old rag doll, pinned up against a couple of moth eaten teddy bears and guarded by some rusty tin soldiers. We were all crushed together on top of each other. It was no way to treat a valuable, antique model car.

One day I heard an interesting noise. Someone was coming into the loft. They had climbed the rickety old loft ladder, opened the hatch and they were coming in. "This loft needs clearing," a deep voice moaned. "There's a lot of junk up here and we'll have to order a skip." I was getting nervous. I wasn't sure what was happening. It had been such a long time since anyone had come up here. Why was this happening now? A short man, with greyish hair, started to sort through the boxes. "I'm not joking, there's an incredible amount of junk up here Maureen," he repeated loudly. "The last owner left everything behind." I'd just got used to the idea, that the house had new owners, when his hairy hand unsealed my own box, lifted the lid and rummaged through the contents. He grabbed me with a firm grip. Now it dawned on me that he was throwing the contents of the loft out through the loft hatch. Was that to be my fate? Yes! Before I knew it, I was carelessly dropped out and found myself falling down through space at an alarmingly fast speed and just as I was preparing myself for the impact of landing on the hard floor, a large jolly woman caught me in her arms.

"This is interesting George," I heard a woman's voice say. "It has the original box and it could be valuable." She peered into my box and smoothed her fingers tenderly over my shiny paint work, before wrapping me tightly in a thick covering of bubble wrap. She placed me on the hall table. I didn't have to wait long to see what would happen next. A few hours later, I was taken out to a very strange looking modern car and transported at great speed to an auction room in a place called London. There, I was put on a display stand at the end of a stately hall, in front of an odd collection of human beings, holding catalogues. A round faced man with twinkling blue eyes was holding a hammer. He started the bidding, "Lot 25... I'll start the bidding at £250... £300... Who'll give me £350 for this fine model car, manufactured in 1932?" Some bidders kept raising their hands and to my amazement, the money kept going up, up, up. The hammer went down. I sold for an incredible five hundred pounds. I felt immensely proud, I felt as proud as a lion, I felt as proud as a peacock. Now I stand in pride of place in my new home, a smart glass cabinet in a fashionable town house in Chelsea. I have realised a dream now. I have been repaired. I am part of a collection and I am enjoying the company of my new friends.

Imagine that you are some kind of object or an old toy...

- What could you be?
- Where are you?
- Why are you there?
- How do you feel?

- Imagine someone finds you or does something to you.
- What could it be?
- Tell the story of your adventure

- How is your situation resolved?
- How does the story end?
- How do you feel now?

Use different words and phrases to start sentences. Join ideas with connectives. You can use these examples to help you, but it is better to write your own version.

- From the depths of the loft I cried...
- My previous owners had...

    so I had...

- My paint was ... and...
- I was pushed up against...
- It was no way to treat...

- One day I heard a...
- A deep voice said, "..."
- He started to throw down some of the...
- Suddenly. I was falling through... and I landed with a...

- A woman opened my box and examined me...
- She said, "..."
- They put me in ... and took me to...
- A small boy saw me at the auction and he asked his dad to...
- Then...

    so the boy...

- Now I am a ... which is...

Now write about some older people you know.

My great, great grandma is very old, but she is always kind, loving and thoughtful. She sings me songs that she learnt when she was young and tells me stories about (her childhood) the good old days when she was a child.

Remember Great uncle Arthur who sits in his chair by the window. He never stops grumbling and complaining. He hides behind the curtain and he waits for children to pick the flower heads from his garden, so he can bang on the window at them.

Imagine you are an elderly person living in 2090.

Are you eighty or even ninety or even a hundred and something?	Do you have any wrinkles on your face?	Are you crippled up with pain because you have arthritis?
Do you have a walking frame? Do you have a mobility scooter?	Do you shuffle and limp? Do you walk with a stick?	What are you like?
Are you kind, smiling and friendly?	Are you a complaining, grumbling and thoughtless person?	Are you caring and considerate?
Do you love being surrounded by your grandchildren and talking to them?	What do your remember from long ago? *(the old fashioned cars, the large mobile phones and i pads).*	Are you trapped in a small flat?
Are you unable to walk far because you are in a wheelchair?	How do you feel?	

I am quite sad and lonely, but I cheer up when people call.

Write this fantasy story set in a different time zone. Write one of your own.

Now, imagine *life's* changed.

Setting:
it's 2090
early morning
story takes place in a computerised home in the future
in an underground city full of gadgets

Character:
you are an old man of one hundred and four years old
sad, lonely and bored
crippled up with pain because you have arthritis
no exercise
your hands are shaky

Plot:
- you press the screen to operate the computer to programme in your daily needs
- nothing happens – the screen has gone black
- a dreaded power cut has occurred
- all the machines in the flat are dead

What happens next?
- life cannot continue without the machines
- you feel lost and fearful
- you try to remember what life was like when you were young
- when you used to go outside into the sun
- go shopping in the High Street to get provisions
- play football
- you will die of hunger if you stay here in your underground home.
- Suddenly, you have an idea.
- you try to stand
- stumble awkwardly across the dark room and fumble for the key to turn the lock which hasn't been used for years
- the door opens and you step into the elevator

How does it end?
- it still works – it goes up, up, up
- you arrive at the surface
- and step INTO DAYLIGHT – the first time for 50 years
- you feel the fresh air on your skin
- you are free from your prison
- in the distance you see...

Now, write the story.

At 6.45am I slowly sat up, wiped the sleepy dust from my eyes and I typed into my lap top computer my getting up programme, but nothing happened. The computer had crashed. How would I fold my bed into the wall, get out my chair and order my meals for the day. I felt...

Now, it's your turn to write some stories. We are going to think about how you can build up characters, settings and plots.

What is my setting?	Who are my characters?	How do you feel?
- at the park/forest	- auntie	- stunned - horrified
- at the canal	- uncle	- dazed - frightened
- at the riverbank/lake	- grandad	- fearful - upset
- at the seaside	- grandma	- petrified - shaken
- in outer space	- mum/step-mum	- terrified - distressed
- in a plane	- dad/step-dad	- shocked - anxious
- in a ship or submarine	- friends	- astonished - traumatised
	- strangers	- disgusted - surprised

What is my plot? Is there a problem or complication that triggers some action? How does the plot develop?

- People sun bathing on patterned towels on the beach, but a toddler wanders into the sea alone.	- Children playing games in the park: rugby, football, tennis and cricket, but someone gets hit in the face by a ball.	- You are feeding the ducks, Canada Geese and swans, but you see an injured cygnet, which has a fish hook hanging from its mouth.
- A lady is sailing in her yacht, but she falls over board.	- A dark shadow is seen in the water and it is moving rapidly towards the bathers. Could it be a shark?	- A boy, on holiday, is having fun sailing in his inflatable dinghy, but he gets into trouble in deep water.
- Children are paddling in the shallow water, but what are those lumps of jelly? HELP! Could they be poisonous jellyfish?	- You fall asleep on the beach and you get badly sun burnt.	- You leave your clothes on the beach while you swim in the sea, but when you come back they are gone. Have they been stolen?
- You are swimming, when you see an enormous wave on the horizon, but can you get to safety in time?	- You are travelling on a train, when it breaks down in a tunnel. How do you get out of the tunnel?	- You walk in the park, but your dog tramples the flower bed and the park attendant is approaching angrily.

- You walk in the forest, but there is a huge thunderstorm and torrential rain.

- You get stung by an insect or bitten by a snake, but are you allergic?

- You climb up the rocks on the side of a cliff, but you lose your nerve.

- You are walking in the national park and you hear a ferocious roar behind you. Is it a bear?

- You are flying to your holiday destination, when a man stands up and attempts to hijack the plane.

- You take a ride on the roller coaster or a wheel, but it breaks down and you get stuck at the top.

- You are walking in the forest, when you see black smoke and flames coming from the bushes. Is it a forest fire?

- You walk your dog in the park, but he gets lost.

- You walk in the country, but a furious bull chases you. Can you make it to the gate?

- You go for a walk on the moor, but a mist comes down and you can't see the path that leads to the car park.

- Your purse or wallet is stolen when you are on holiday and you have to sleep on a park bench.

- You are on a cruise but there is a huge storm at sea. Is the boat grounded? Does it hit a rock? Does it capsize or sink? Are the people rescued?

- You are climbing inside a warplane in the museum and suddenly you find yourself in a real battle. Have you gone back in time?

- You are staying in your caravan, when the river bursts its banks and you are floating in deep water.

- You stand on a sharp object and have to find a doctor.

- You go on a long trek, but you get blisters and can't go on.

- Your truck breaks down in the desert and you have to stay the night there.

- You are walking through the town centre, when you are grabbed from behind. Is it a kidnapper?

- You are on a space rocket, but there is a technical problem and you have to make an emergency landing on a strange planet. Will the aliens be friendly?

- You are travelling in a submarine, miles beneath the ocean, but the warning siren is ringing and water is coming in.

Can you think of any more plots? Sometimes it helps to describe things that have actually happened to you, but why not let your imagination run wild? *(Remember do not make your story too far fetched.)*

Build up suspense. Reach a crisis point.
You end up:

- swimming for your life
- alerting everyone to the danger
- diving in to rescue
- being winched into a helicopter by rope
- overpowering your attacker.
- calling desperately for help
- phoning the emergency services for help
- walking through a dark tunnel
- searching all night
- sending up a a flare
- radioing for help
- clambering on to the life raft
- finding shelter

What happens next? How is the problem resolved?

You can be rescued by:	*You can:*	*How do you feel when you are rescued?*
- a life guard	- flee	- relieved
- a stranger on the beach	- run	- thankful
- a life boat	- avoid	- happy to be alive
- a helicopter or air ambulance	- make a hasty retreat	- appreciative
- the mountain rescue team	- bolt	- grateful
- fire brigade	- escape	- glad
- police officer	- make a get away	- cheerful
- army	*You speak on or to:*	- lucky
- member of family	- T.V	- fortunate
- You can use all of your own strength to get out of a situation	- local radio	- thrilled
You have to go to:	- newspaper	- in high spirits
- hospital	- someone in authority	- emotional
- first aid or medical tent	- magazine	- traumatised

Mrs Barker, the teacher says, "Let's write and write and write about anything and everything. We have been writing stories. These are also called narratives (fiction). Now let's write non-fiction."

> Non-fiction writing can be the form of:
> - newspaper reports
> - accident reports
> - school reports
> - instructions
> - interviews
> - leaflets
> - diaries
> - recounts
> - travel writing
> - letters and arguments
> - biographies and auto biographies

First you must decide **who your reader is** and **who your audience are**. You need to know if you should write in a formal way, like a news report, or in a chatty informal style - as to a friend.

1. If you are writing to an important person or adult you don't know, your writing should be formal.

    I am very concerned that

2. If you are writing to an adult (you know well) or another child, you can write informally.

    Hi,
    Just wanted to say...

Organise **NON-FICTION**

Use a diagram and label it.

One of the BIGGEST Mammals on earth.

The largest members of the beaked whale family.

They are a protected species.

The rare northern Bottlenose Whale

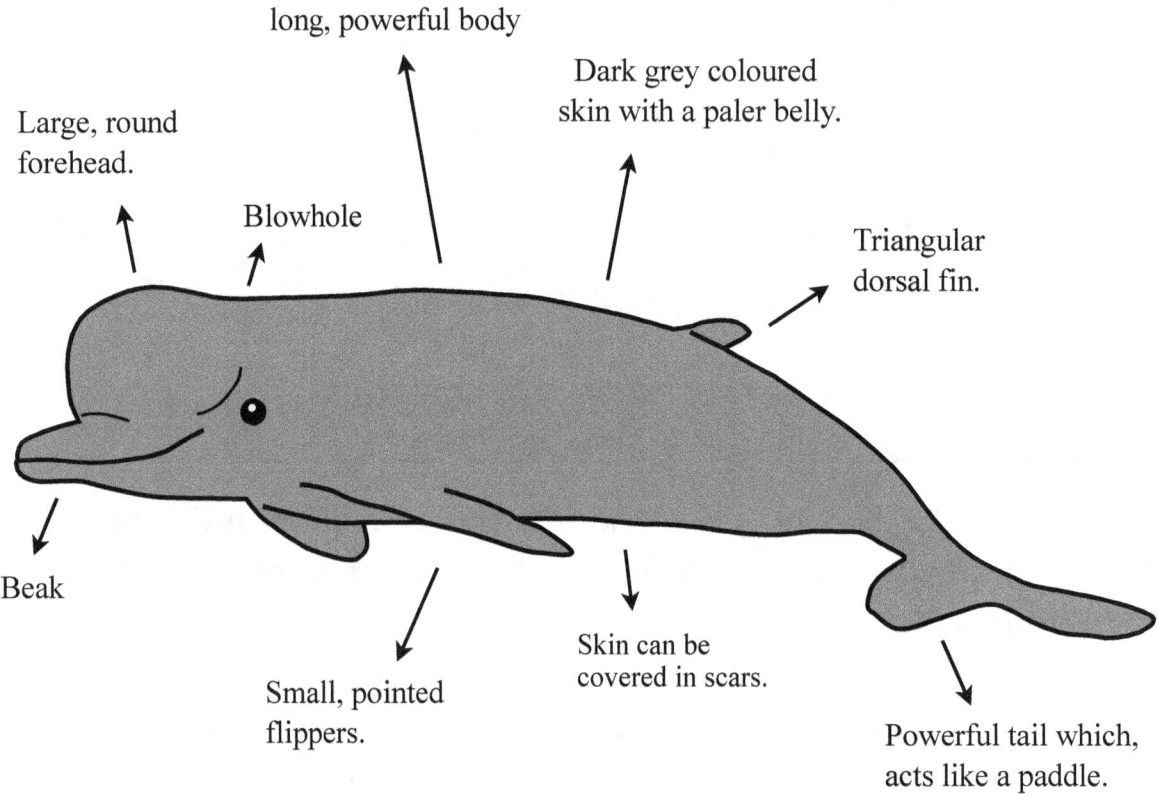

- long, powerful body
- Large, round forehead.
- Blowhole
- Dark grey coloured skin with a paler belly.
- Triangular dorsal fin.
- Beak
- Small, pointed flippers.
- Skin can be covered in scars.
- Powerful tail which, acts like a paddle.

DIET	**BEHAVIOUR**	**FACTS**
- squid	- inquisitive	- live for up to 40 years
- fish	- acrobatic	- dive to at least 1500 metres
- starfish	- live in schools.	- adults can grow to 9.8 metres in length
- prawns	- social	- can stay underwater for up to 2 hours

Look up the Northern Bottlenose Whale. Add information.

Use a table so your reader can find information quickly.

Species:	
Located in:	Atlantic Ocean, off the coast of Scotland.
Size:	
Colour & Appearance	Range from dark grey to olive brown with a paler coloured belly. They are often covered in scars and marks.
Food:	
Life Span:	30-40 years on average.
Young:	Called calves

Complete the chart.

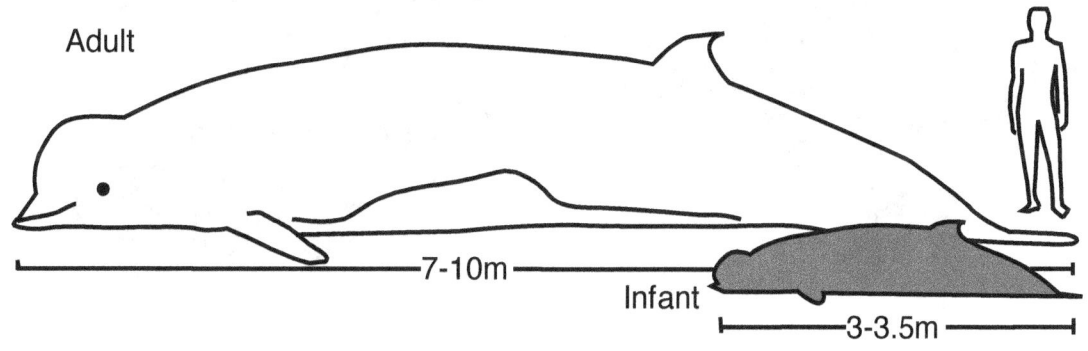

Make a list of different kinds of whales:

- the blue whale
- the killer whale
- ....
- ....
- ....
- ....

Find out some facts about one of them - appearance, diet, behaviour.

Present your information in a diagram using:

- Headings
- Subheadings
- Text Boxes
- Pictures
- Different fonts
- Punctuation

Now make a table so your reader can find information quickly.

Your non-fiction writing must have:

- an introduction
- several points written in paragraphs
- conclusion with a comment from the author

Use boxes to display information - for fast fact finding.

Make an information leaflet on Northern Bottlenose Whales. Can you find anymore information?

Northern <u>Bottlenose</u> Whale

Where is this whale found?

The northern bottlenose whale is found in deep water. It swims off the ....
....
....
....

What does it look like?

The whale has a huge black body which measures .... It is sleek, streamlined and shiny with a dark triangular fin.

Does it communicate?

- makes loud noises
- gives out whistle like sounds
- can be heard kilometres away by other whales
- a mother can communicate with her baby and find it if it wanders away.
- it uses a sonar navigation device called echolocation to help find a food sauce.

What does it eat?

- shrimp
- squid

Is it in danger?

- yes
- it is hunted illegally
- whale hunting was banned in 1992

How does it move?

- swims fast
- dives deep
- arches its back like a dolphin
- flips its tail
- surfaces for air
- spurts a puff of spume from its blow hole.

Write sentences using these notes.

Use **BOLD HEADLINES**, <u>Subheadings</u> and different fonts.

HEADLINE GRABS READER'S ATTENTION   DATE

A WHALE OF A TIME

Presenting a Newspaper Report

| STRAPLINE tells you more about the story and makes reader read on. | DIFFERENT SIZE FONTS MAKE WORDS STAND OUT. |

A **WHALE** Swam up the **River Thames**

Subheading

By Anya Smith

1. The first paragraph **sums up** the news story. Ask...

WHERE	River Thames
WHEN	21st January
WHY	Got lost
WHO	Whale
WHICH	Bottlenose whale

   HUNDREDS OF PEOPLE WATCH
   SUBHEADING BREAKS UP THE TEXT TO MAKE IT EASY TO READ.

2. Give more details in short paragraphs of one or two sentences.

   - Use good emotive words, adjectives and powerful verbs.
   - Use alliteration
     What a wonderful whale.
   - Use similes, metaphors

   > Newspaper text is written in columns.
   >
   > It is written in the third person and all tenses are used.
   >
   > Short paragraphs of one or two sentences are used.

Photo helps reader understand the story.

Picture: Caption explains the photo

3. Include a quotation from an eyewitness.

   "I couldn't believe my eyes when I saw a whale in the river"

   Tommy Flynn said, "They were splashing the whale with water"

   This is **DIRECT** SPEECH.

   You can use **REPORTED** SPEECH.

   Environmentalist John Curtis stated that he was concerned about the safety of the whale.

4. Give some more background information. What is it like in the Atlantic Ocean - the Whales usual habitat?

5. End with:
   - A personal opinion or comment from the author.
   - Link the event to one like it.
   - Consider what might happen next.
   - Ask a rhetorical question and answer it.

   Will the whale survive? No one knows! The next four days will be crucial but we will have to wait and see what will happen.

A WHALE OF A TIME

WHALE WAITS AS IT GETS STRANDED ON BEACH.

By Anya Smith

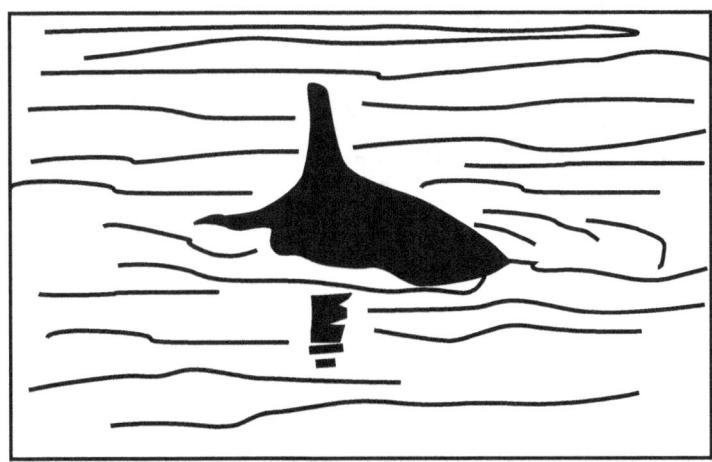
Picture: Whale in the Thames

On January 20th, a rare Northern Bottlenose whale, swam up the River Thames in London and landed by Battersea Bridge. The whale was lost. He took the wrong direction and instead of swimming out to sea, went down the Thames.

The whale caused major traffic jams, because hundreds of people lined the bank of the Thames in London to see him. It was such an unusual sight to see a whale swimming up the Thames.

Challenges

However, as he swam upstream, past the Houses of Parliament, against the falling tide, wildlife experts became increasingly worried about his safety.

Natalie Smith - a leading marine biologist, who flew in from the USA as soon as she heard the news stated, "I splashed him to keep him afloat. Then I waved my arms and shouted, 'Go back,' to stop him landing on the banks of the river. I knew he would be safer in the water. I think he understood me."

Mrs Tucker, an eyewitness, explained, "I was travelling on a train over the river, when I spotted a whale swimming slowly under the Tower Bridge. I couldn't believe my eyes, so I phoned the police."

Tommy Flynn said, "My family came straight down to London when we saw it on T.V. because we would never get another chance to see something like this."

LEADING MARINE BIOLOGIST NATALIE SMITH SPEAKS OUT.

Northern Bottlenose whales are usually found in deep water in the North Atlantic Ocean off the coast of Canada or Scotland. Experts believe the whale lost its direction, because something went wrong with its sonar navigation system.

Will the whale be saved? If it can be persuaded to swim up the river, back into open sea, it will survive. If it can't swim, experts will do some tests on him.

What is a fact?

FACTS are TRUE

Whales swim with granny, their mums and her other children. They are a school. **True or False?**

Facts are true because there is **evidence** to prove it.

Whales are the largest mammals.

What is an opinion?

Opinions are what a writer believes.

It may not be what other people think.

Whales are beautiful creatures.

Sometimes you'll find an opinion in a fact.

A beautiful creature swam up the River Thames.

Are these facts or opinions?

Whales are everyone's favourite animal.

Whales are inquisitive creatures.

Whales communicate by a sonar navigation system called echolocation.

Whales can hold their breath for 10 minutes under water.

A whale can weigh as much as 30 elephants.

The whale swam up the river because it took a wrong turning.

Another whale was seen in the Thames in 1899.

Let's write to **persuade**.

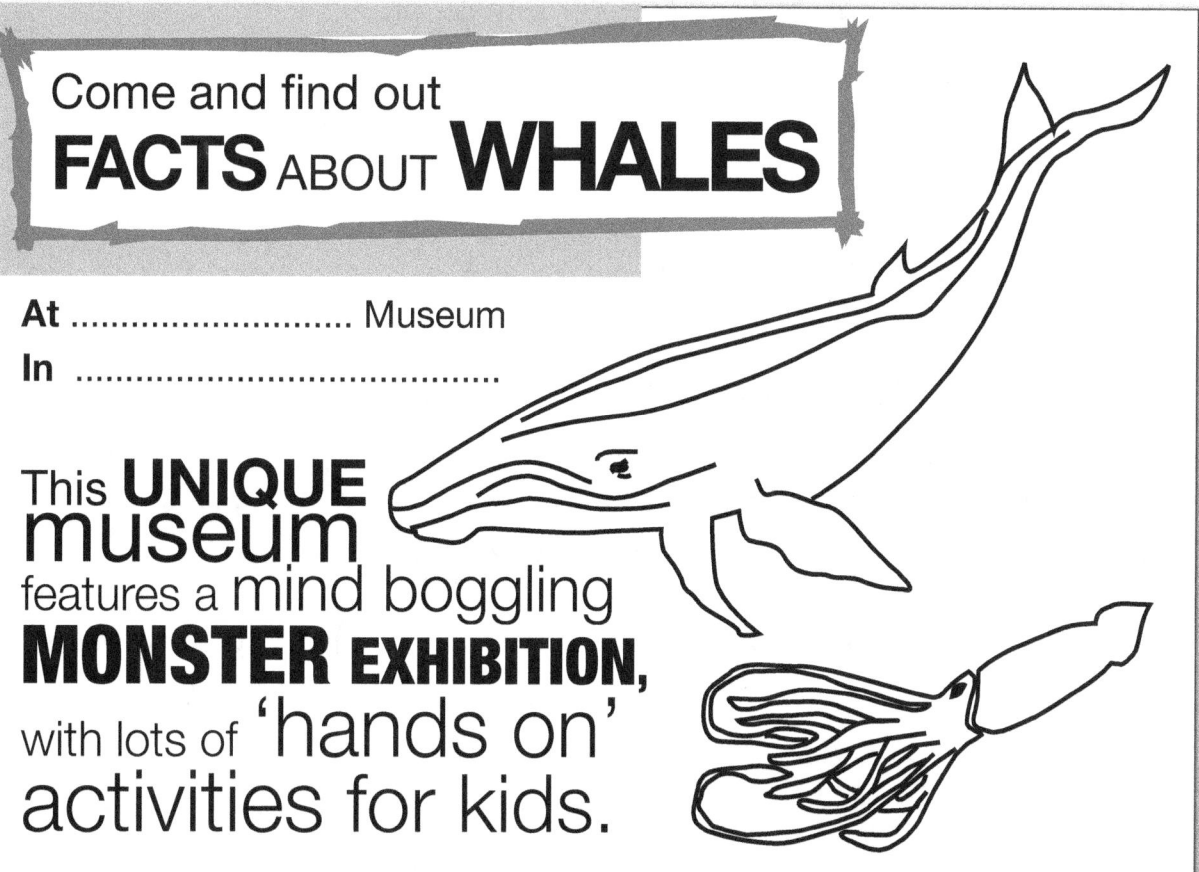

Come and find out FACTS ABOUT WHALES

At .... Museum

In ....

This **UNIQUE** museum features a mind boggling **MONSTER EXHIBITION**, with lots of 'hands on' activities for kids.

Come and explore our life size model of a Blue Whale and discover what it would be like to be swallowed by the largest of deep ocean creatures.

You enter the massive monster through the door marked entrance. Now follow the arrows around.

Inside the gigantic mouth

You discover there are no teeth at all. Instead there are some stringy plates that hang down from the jaw. You watch the monstrous whale gulp in huge mouthfuls of sea water. He filters out some food: tasty krill (small creatures like shrimp that live on the seabed) and other small creatures.

The Tongue

Now you dodge the terrifying tongue as it comes down to lick its stringy plates so he can swallow down all the food that is trapped there.

The Throat

Next, you slide down a flume but you're not at the pool. You're sliding down the monsters massive throat with the krill. The monster has closed his mouth so it is very dark.

Escape Route

The walls around you start to shake. You find yourself travelling faster and faster back up the tubes. The whale spits you out on the beach in the museum.

The Noise

Deep down in the monster's stomach you hear the whale's song, his echolocation. His whistle like sound is louder than an aircraft engine. He uses it to communicate with other whales and hunt for food. It's deafening; you cover your ears as you follow the route round.

The Stomach

A sphere ball awaits you. You get in and roll rapidly down a tunnel, that leads to the monster's stomach. You're surrounded by the deadly acid of his digestive juices.

If you get out alive – you can experience our 'Virtual Whale Experience': you can swim with a whale, blowing out spume, hunting with the school and catching prey.

Next, you can have a go at being a marine biologist. Dive deep with the whales – in our specially adapted 'ocean buggy' simulator. Get alongside the whales in their natural environment, where it is dark and dingy and the water is murky at the bottom of the ocean.

By the time you get back on dry land, you'll be ravenously hungry. End your visit by eating in our whale themed restaurant and enjoy a whale burger with a delicious squid coke.

Can't wait to see you there.

Recount

You went on a school trip to the Monster Exhibition.

On .... at ...., I went to the ....
....

You will see huge creatures like ....
....

The exhibition teaches you a lot of facts about whales. You learn about their colour, their shape and ....
.... You also learn that .... by watching D.V.Ds and playing games on computers.

First I went for a walk inside the whale experience. The journey starts as you enter the whales mouth ....
....
....

Secondly, ...
....
....
....

Thirdly, ...
....
....

After this, I went on the whale simulator and travelled to ....
....
....

Finally, I tried some delicious .... in the ....
....

I thought it was amazing because...
....
....

South Sands BEACH RESCUE

I'm from the Beach Rescue Team. You're probably wondering why I'm writing to you. Well if you've been to South Sea beach you've probably seen the guys in red T-shirts on the beach.

I'm really proud of these guys who patrol the beach to keep your children safe, while they play or swim on the seashore. I'm just as proud of the men in the red helicopters, who cruise the coast looking for people who have got into trouble at sea.

Let me describe a typical day as a member of the Beach Rescue team. Out at sea, a young teenager, Jo had fallen overboard from her uncle's yacht. When we reached her, she was clinging on to the safety line in treacherously rough water. If we had arrived a few minutes later, she would have been too tired to hold on. We took her back to shore and she was taken to hospital in a waiting ambulance. We saved her life that day.

WHAT WE NEED:

- Kit
- Helicopter
- Jet Ski Boats
- Training
- Member Packs
- Activity Packs for children

We are really busy so we need your help. If we run out of money we won't be able to do all the emergency calls we're called out to every day.

If you put £5 in an envelope and send it to us, you will help our voluntary workers save the lives of people like Jo.

BEACH RESCUE IS A CHARITY SO PLEASE GIVE GENEROUSLY

Tips and techniques on how to write to persuade or to make your reader believe in something.

<u>Make a point, provide evidence to support it, comment to reinforce your view.</u>

- use emotive words, like powerful adjectives
- use alliteration
- appeal directly to your reader
- use rhetorical questions
- use an anecdote or little story
- repeat words
- use a catchy slogan

Instructions

SHARK ALERT WARNING NOTICE

HIGH RISK AREA
DO NOT BATHE IN THE SEA
DO NOT SURF
SWIM AT OWN RISK

KEEP TO THE OFFICIAL SWIMMING POOL

Tip (The Imperative)
Instructions tell us what to do. They must be set out clearly in a list. Use bullet points to list your short points.

---

1. How many bossy words (imperatives) can you find?

    KEEP TO...

2. Can you make up some more instructions. Write about:

    litter, lighting fires or having barbecues, bikes, dogs or any more you can think of...

3. Look for other writing that explains how to do things.

    For example, a cooking recipe

SOUTH SANDS POLICE DEPARTMENT
POLICE REPORT

Case No: 6005432

Date: September 4th 2024

Reporting Officer: Dan Stevens

Witness: Sophia Lewis

Incident: Car broken into

On Wednesday the 9th June, we climbed the steep hill to the cliff tops, where the car was parked. It was about 10pm. As my dad put the key in the lock, I heard his shout that the car had been broken into. The window had been smashed in with a heavy object and there was glass all over the seats and on the floor. Our designer holdall had been stolen, some jackets and our collection of C.D.s.

As Dad phoned 999, a police car arrived because somebody had already reported the incident. He examined the crime scene and recorded down some notes in his book. Then he said we must come down to the station to make a statement. Next, the policeman told my sisters and I to jump into the police car and we drove off at top speed with the lights flashing.

After this, we went to a small interview room where we answered lots of questions. The policeman made more notes, but my dad couldn't remember all the things we had in the car. Then the phone rang. It was another policeman phoning to say that our bags had been found. They were lying behind a bush in the gardens of some flats, where they'd been thrown. The contents were all there. He said that a witness had seen some youths break into the car and steal the goods. They ran off down the road, but a passing boy chased them. It appears they were so frightened that they dropped the loot and ran off.

Give ONLY the FACTS. Make them clear. Use FORMAL WRITING.

1. Now write the policeman's report about the incident.

   For example: *I was called to ..... at ...... on..... I saw a ... with its windows completely smashed...*

2. Now write the witnesses report. Write what he saw and how he chased the thieves. Describe where, when, how, what the thieves looked like and what happened.

   For example: *It was shortly after... when I heard the sound of breaking glass... and saw three youths making off with... I shouted... As they legged it up the road I...*

3. The thieves are caught. Write the statement from the thieves' view point. Do they admit they are guilty of the crime?

   For example: *At ten o'clock I was at a fish and chip shop across the road...*

Simon keeps a diary so he can record what he does and how he feels in the future.

Let's peep into his entry for April 19th...

I get so bored when my family go shopping on Saturday. We trail round the same shops and there's so much hanging around – so if I see something interesting I pick it up and read it. I saw an interesting leaflet advertising a competition this afternoon. It says it wants you to write a slogan of not more than twenty words, to say why YIKE trainers are better than other brands. Well, I don't know if they are or not, but I think I'll have a go anyway. I haven't got anything else to do here.

I take the entry back to Dad, while we wait for my Mum and sister to look round the department. We stand by the counter and try out lots of different sentences with only 20 words. We scribble it over and over again - turning words round – until we are satisfied that our sentence sounds good – really good – excellent – the best. Then we put it in the entry box.

April 28th

Imagine my surprise! The phone rings. I pick it up and it's the lady from Y.I.K.E trainers. She tells me that I have won a brand new pair of cool Y.I.K.E trainers, because I wrote the best slogan.
"Y.I.K.E trainers," I scream, "YIPPEEE...."
"I have always wanted a pair. Thank you so much." She says that she will put them in the post. I am ecstatic because soon, I will be walking round in my new designer trainers. Shopping doesn't seem half so bad now.

Luke writes a project in his school holiday and records his thoughts about it in his diary. Shall we peep into it?

April 14th

My Dad brought home a magazine with a competition in it today. You have to write a project on an environmental theme. I couldn't decide whether to enter, but I decided to give it a go. What should I write about? I've done 'Saving The Planet' and 'The Rain Forest' at school this term. I didn't want to research 'Pollution' or 'Saving Energy' or 'Recycling', because it sounds like a lot of work in the holiday – so I decided to write about the tree at the bottom of my garden

July 2oth

That tree is amazing. It has stood in view of my bedroom window all these years, but I didn't realise how much I could learn from it. I went on the internet to research loads of scientific facts about how trees make food to feed themselves, using a process called photosynthesis.

July 24th

I discovered that it is a habitat for a whole host of different life forms including:

- insect species
- bird life
- tiny mammals
- fungus

Write down some facts that Luke can put in his project. Draw the tree and label it with facts.

July 3oth

I took a series of photos of my tree and did some bark rubbings, which I have stuck in beside my writing.

August 8th

Mum posted my project this morning. I can't wait to see if I win.

September 4th

It is 8.30 am in the morning. I've just arrived all sleepy eyed at school – my teacher picks me out. Oh no, I think, what have I done? He grins from one side of his face to the other.

"You've won a national competition," he beams, "You're off to a top hotel to be presented with your prize by a celebrity. You've won a holiday for yourself and one thousand pounds worth of books for the school.

"Well done!" I couldn't believe it. I was so excited, but then I thought, I will have to go out in front of assembly.

October 1st

....

....

....

....

Write a diary entry for the day he collects his prize. What does he win? Who presents it?

What will Stephen's head teacher say about his achievement to the school in assembly? Write a report for the school magazine

Now you have a go:

- If you could win a competition like Frank, what would you like to win and why? What did you have to do to win it? Who would you like to present the prize?

Imagine you have entered a competition. Write the letter you received telling you that you'd won first prize. Make sure you include details about the prize.

- How do you feel as you open and read the letter?

- What is the first thing you do?

> **"Let's write some letters.**
>
> Lets write to inform... to complain... to explain... to argue... to describe... to persuade and to advise. Lets write to say thank you...,"
>
> says Mrs Barker.

Which letters are formal and which are informal?

Mrs Barker says business letters must be **formal**. They must not use slang or casual words. They must have the formal language that news readers use.

If a letter starts with 'Dear Sir' you use 'Yours faithfully' to end it. If a letter starts with 'Dear Mr or Mrs…' you must use 'Yours sincerely'. Letters to our friends can be informal and they can use casual words and end in 'love from.'

Write all letters in three paragraphs. Remember P.E.C:

P	**P**	make a **POINT**
E	**E**	show **EVIDENCE**
C	**E**	always **COMMENT** or give **EXPLANATION**

Mrs Barker is angry, that the council are knocking down the local outdoor swimming pool to build a ring road round the town. She gets her class to write some letters to the council.

> The children have been learning how to write an argument with 2 sides. They put forward:
>
> - their own point of view,
> - the **opposite point of view**.
>
> ...as they argue against the council's proposed road scheme.

Read the following letters. Underline the arguments against building the ring road in red and the opposite viewpoint in blue. Each letter shows a different way to write an argument.

- Introduce your point of view, give some evidence and explain it.
- Present the counter argument or opposite point of view.
- Use linking words or conjunctions to join paragraphs.
- Sum up with some comments.

---

2 Cherry Orchard,
Rushford,
RG21 6FG.

The Complaints Manager,
Rushford Council,
15 High Street,
Rushford.
RG21 7AD.

Dear Sir or Madam,

I am writing to express my concern about the council's plan to knock down our swimming pool to make way for the new bypass. Local people are asking this question. Why does the road have to be built on the swimming pool site? Surely, it would be more beneficial to the people of Rushford if the swimming pool remained open. At this early stage, the council can change the proposed route of the bypass and build the road further out in the countryside, which will mean there will be less pollution in the town.

The people of Rushford really value that pool. It was opened over one hundred years ago by our present Queen's grandfather. Since that time, it has been used each summer by thousands of people. They come to learn to swim, to enjoy splashing in the pool or just relax by the pool side in the sun. Alternatively, they come to join in exercise classes in the gym. If the pool closes these people will have nowhere to go because it is a long journey to the nearest leisure centre. If the road plans go ahead, Rushford will have lost a piece of history.

More than this, the swimming pool cafe has a reputation for serving good food. People come for miles just to have a cup of coffee and meet with their friends. Where will these people go, especially elderly people, if the plans go ahead? Finally, the pool is needed because it is a large venue, which has room for many people. It is used for concerts, discos and even weddings. We cannot do without this pool. The people of Rushford need this pool. I would be glad to hear your comments.

Yours faithfully,

Toby

Toby introduces the council's viewpoint and then argues against it.

> Kitty introduces three of the council viewpoints and argues against them.

2 Lucan Drive,
Rushford,
RG15 3ER

The Complaints Manager,
Rushford Council,
15 High Street,
Rushford.
RG21 7AD.

Dear Sir or Madam,

I am concerned that the council are planning to knock down our pool because they say it is too expensive to maintain (to run). This is ridiculous! Hundreds of local people flock to the pool during the summer months and they would be willing to pay a few more pence to enter, rather than lose their pool. The council have also wasted so much money rebuilding the council offices, when they could have spent the money on the pool.

As well as this, the council say that it is more important to spend money building a new bypass (a main road) rather than modernising an old swimming pool. The people of this town do not want any more road improvement schemes. Besides, if drivers and their passengers travel round the outside of the town in their cars, they will not come into the town centre to spend money in the shops. If shop keepers do not sell much, their shops will close. The museums will also close. The town will be deserted, a ghost town (a metaphor), like other towns where there are bypasses. It is clearly better to spend the money on improving facilities at the old pool.

Finally, the council inform us that the local people do not want the old, out dated, outside pool. They say that the water is too cold and the majority of people would prefer to go to the luxurious leisure centre at Raines, five miles away, where there is a heated indoor swimming pool. This is certainly not the case because answers to a recent survey showed that people love to dive in the refreshing cold water on a summer's day and relax in the sun by the pool side. They do not want to have to fill their cars up with expensive petrol and travel miles to an indoor complex that is also crowded, chaotic and noisy. I am therefore appealing to you to reconsider these proposals and look forward to hearing from you.

Yours faithfully,

Kitty

---

13 Christopher Court,
Rushford,
RG45 4HJ.

The Complaints Manager,
Rushford Council,
15 High Street,
Rushford.
RG21 7AD.

Dear Councillors,

I am extremely dissatisfied to hear about the councils latest proposal to knock down our swimming pool, so a new by pass can be built. You say the building is unsightly (an eye saw), because it is old and dilapidated. However, it will cost far more money to build this new road than to modernise the swimming pool. Surely the advantages of having a swimming pool outweigh the benefits of having a new road.

The pool is a popular facility in the summer. It is in the centre of the town, so the majority of people can walk there. It organises swimming lessons for children after school, which means children will be safer when they go near the river. It has a paddling pool for youngsters. It also has swimming lanes twenty metres long, so people can practise swimming lengths in different strokes. Workers can go to the pool before work and swim several lengths so they keep healthy. The local community needs this pool.

You say the new bypass is desperately needed to avoid traffic congestion in the town. You point out that local people will be able to use the new road, in the future, to travel quickly to the huge leisure centre in Raines several miles away. However, this certainly will not be good for the environment. It will increase peoples' carbon footprints; more cars on the road will pollute the countryside with exhaust fumes. It will be inconvenient for: families with young children, teenagers, people who do not own cars, or disabled people - who will be forced to make long expensive journeys on public transport. What would we rather have, a new road or our old pool? I think you know! We ask you to reconsider this proposal.

Yours faithfully,

Farah

> Farah also refers to the councils viewpoint as she argues against it.

Write your own letter to the council. Remember Claudette's Circus. Did you agree or disagree that animals should be kept in circuses. Look at your points again. Write a balanced argument showing that your opinion is right.

Sophia dislikes it when she orders something on- line and:

- it takes weeks to come
- it is broken
- it is not what she ordered

 Write your own letter to complain about something.

French Avenue,
Rushford
RG45 3AG.

Garden Centre,
22 High Street,
Rushford.

Dear Sir or Madam,

I am writing to complain about a bunch of roses I ordered from your company last week for my mum's birthday. On arrival at my house, the rose's petals were already withered because they were nearly dead.

I am also concerned that you did not send me the right colour. I ticked a box to buy yellow roses, but you sent me white ones. Worse than this, the flowers did not arrive on time. I asked for them to be delivered in the morning, but they arrived in the afternoon. My mum had already gone to work so she missed the delivery van and a neighbour had to bring them round later.

In view of this, I was very disappointed with the service I received. This is the first time I have experienced a problem, even though I buy a lot of flowers from your shop. Please can you give me a full refund so I can buy my mum another present.

Yours faithfully,

Sophia

Kayleigh dislikes it when the hospital has closed and she has to travel miles to see a doctor. She writes a letter to her local council to complain.

 Now write another letter to complain about your post office closing.

Clifton Gardens,
North Rushford,
RU15 3AF.

Rushford Council,
15 High Street,
Rushford.
RG21 7AD.

Dear Mrs J. Griffiths,

      I am writing a letter about the proposed closure of the accident and emergency unit at Rushford Hospital on August 3rd. This is a good hospital and I do not think it should close. A year ago my sister broke her leg when she fell off her horse. She had it pinned during an emergency operation at Rushford Hospital and she is still regularly visiting the consultant. She says the doctors and nurses are very kind and care for her well.

Another reason why it should not close down, is because the hospital is next to a busy airport and a web of major motorways with busy traffic. From time to time, there are major accidents and the patients may be badly injured and need to be rushed to a nearby hospital. It has also recently been rebuilt and is a modern building with exquisite facilities. It is next to a large superstore open 24 hours, so visitors to the hospital can buy all their gifts, like flowers and chocolates.

If the accident and emergency department closes it will be a long way to travel to other hospitals and patients will have a longer wait in other hospitals. Their lives could be put at risk. Moreover, the closure of the hospital will mean many people will lose their jobs and it may be difficult for them to get another one.

We need our hospital so please don't close it.

Yours sincerely,

Kayleigh

Leo dislikes spring days when the grass is cut and the pollen makes his sister sneeze, sneeze, sneeze – (no one else likes her sneezing either). He writes a letter asking for help. **Write your own letter asking for something.**

Flat 31,
Foxley Court,
Rushford,
RU15 4FG.

Healthy Days Magazine,
Clear Water Industrial Estate,
Raines,
GH12 6DF.

Dear Sir or Madam,

I wish to reply to your letter which appeared in 'Healthy Days' magazine on 25th July. I was very interested to hear about the help and support you give to people with hay fever.

My sister has severe problems with hay fever. Sometimes her nose is so blocked up that she has to use a whole box of tissues. She can't go outside for fresh air in the summer because her eyes start to water and she starts coughing and sneezing.

I would really like to help my sister with her difficulties so I would like a copy of the booklet 'How To Treat Hay fever'. I would be grateful if you could send it to my address at the top of the letter.

Yours faithfully,

Leo Smith

Shona's granny is hopping mad with the builders working on her house.

17 Church Road,
Rushford,
RG43 4AF.

McNeil Building Contractors,
Rushford Trading Estate,
Rushford,
RG56 356,

Dear Sir or Madam,

I am writing to express my dissatisfaction about the service I am receiving, from your building company, who are building an extension to my kitchen.

When I agreed to have the work carried out, you told me it would take about four weeks to complete. Three months have now gone by and the work is nowhere near finished. Besides this, the builders have left piles of rubbish all over the front garden, which is very dangerous when my grandchildren come round. In fact, I have to keep the children inside in case they fall or injure themselves on a plank of wood or rusty nail.

In conclusion, please can you finish this work by (...) or else I will refuse to pay the invoice. I will have no choice but to call another builder in to finish it.

Yours faithfully,
Olive Mcdonald

Donna's dad is furious about the state of the train.

121 Hengrove Crescent,
Rushford,
RG56 7SD.

Complaints Department,
South West Trains,
Rushford,
RG15 4AS.

Dear Sir or Madam,

I am writing to complain about the train service, from London to Rushford (on... at...). I also want to bring your attention to the deplorable state of your train carriages.

When my train arrived at my destination yesterday evening, it did not stop at the station, but passed through at great speed. Consequently, I had to get off the train at the next station. It took me two hours to walk back to Rushford so I was unable to take my daughter to her piano lesson and so she could not practise for her exam. As well as this, the carriage was filthy and had not been cleaned for days. There were sweet wrappers and crisps all over the floor and chewing gum on the seats. In addition to this, there was a group of unruly teenagers at the end of the carriage, who were behaving badly and causing a disturbance. They clearly did not have tickets, but the ticket inspector just passed them by.

Why should respectable people who have been working hard all day, have to sit in such discomfort. It is shocking. I would be interested to hear your comments about this and hope that you will offer me a refund on my ticket.

Yours faithfully,
Justin Lacey

(George)

"I go all wobbly at the sight of blood, broken bones, plasters, bandages, needles and injections. I'm really not cut out to be a nurse"

(Christabelle)

"You're pathetic."

A listener, Justine, writes a letter to a friend who is in hospital. **Now write a letter to someone in hospital. Fill in the gaps using your own ideas.**

Holly Cottage,
Oxley,
Nr Rushford,
RU34 5TY.

Dear Courtney,

I'm really sorry to hear that you fell off your horse when you were practising for the horse trials last week. I hear that you have broken your leg in two places, which must be very uncomfortable. It makes me feel bad to think of you lying there with your leg pinned. I do hope the doctors and nurses are caring for you and that the meals are not too bad.

Do not worry about school because you are not missing much. I will help you catch up when you get back. In literacy we've read a book called ... and ... In numeracy we've learnt about ... We're meant to do rugby and netball in P.E. this term, but it has been so cold outside that so far we haven't had to go out onto that muddy field. Thank goodness! Last Tuesday our class did assembly on ...

Make the most of your time off. I'll try and visit you soon with a present. I can't wait to see you. We are all thinking of you. The whole class has made you a card and signed it. I know you'll like it. Other class news is ... Try and rest and relax as much as possible.

Love,

Justine

Macie loves helping people – baby sitting, shopping, gardening for elderly people or walking people's dogs. She writes a letter saying she can help. **Now write your own letter to say you have found something.**

Isaac likes school trips. He writes a letter thanking his teacher for his school trip. **Write a thank you letter to your teacher for a school trip.**

---

451 Sherwood Road,
Rushford,
RU34 6TY.

Dear Miss Martin,

I found a purse on the floor of the Fresco supermarket, at Rushford on Friday afternoon. It had slipped down the shelf and was hidden under some loaves of bread in the bakery. When I was choosing bread, I saw a brightly coloured object sticking out, so I picked it up.

The purse was made of red leather and opens like a wallet. It has several compartments inside. There was a twenty pound note in the purse and several pound coins. On the back of a card, I found your name, address and telephone number, which is why I'm writing to you.

Please contact me on my mobile phone, 07971 343134 or by e-mail at Macie@hahaa.co.uk to arrange a time to collect your purse. I am in every afternoon after 4.30pm, except Thursday when I go to my piano lesson. I look forward to hearing from you.

Yours sincerely,
Macie

Beech Oaks,
Upper Rushford Road,
Rushford,

Dear Mrs Barker,

I want to thank you for organising such an exciting school trip. Everyone in the class said it was the best one they'd ever been on. The centre was amazing; the beds and dormitories were really comfy and the food in the restaurant was absolutely delicious. We wanted the trip to go on longer.

It was great fun camping in the forest overnight and cooking our breakfast on a camp fire. We learnt so many important skills that will help us in the future - like working in a team. Most of all, I liked the assault course, and climbing the rock face. I had to challenge myself to go up there and jump down on the rope, because I'm scared of heights, but I was really pleased with myself when I had done it.

My holiday project is coming on well. I have stuck in all the photographs I took on the week. They're really good. I have also pressed some wild flowers, leaves and feathers I collected, which I will mount in my book.

Thanks again,

Isaac

Alana loves kind people who invite her to tea or to stay. She likes holidays by the sea.

She writes a letter thanking a relative for inviting her. **Write your own letter to a relative thanking them for a holiday. Fill in the gaps using your own ideas.**

> **An informal letter to a friend can use slang words or informal language. It can end 'Love from.'**

The Vicarage,
Rushford Lane,
Rushford.

Dear Auntie and Uncle,

I am writing to say how much I enjoyed my holiday in ... On Sea. You live in such a pretty seaside resort and the view from your apartment is amazing. Thank you for taking time off work to take me to so many places. It was exciting to go out in uncle's boat round the bay. I also enjoyed swimming in the sea every day. My swimming has really improved and I can swim on my back now.

Mum and Dad were very impressed with my collection of shells. I've made a display of them in my bedroom and I'm going to use them to make some pretty decorations to sell at my school fair. My parents enjoyed looking at the postcards, which I bought and they would like to visit the old historic manor house when they come and visit you.

The term has started now, so I am back in a school routine. I get up at 7pm to ... I have a new teacher called ... We are studying ... I have gone up a group into ... We are practising for a school concert ... / We are preparing for a school trip ... Thank you once again for a wonderful time. I hope to see you again soon.

Love from,

Alana

Aaron loves birthdays. He writes a birthday thank you letter to a friend.

 Now write a birthday thank you letter of your own.

The Old School House,
Oxley,
Rushford

Dear Uncle Nick,

      Thank you for my birthday present, which arrived in the post this morning. It was very kind of you to send me such a cool, new designer pencil case and set of pens. They are just what I need for school as we are doing lots of projects this year and will be so useful. My old pencil case was also so tatty and everyone will be envious when they see my new bright, shiny one.

On my birthday we went ten pin bowling at the leisure centre. I took six friends and we played two games. I managed to score two strikes, by knocking all the pins down, so my team won. After this, we went to the fast food place and had a hamburger and chips, a big glass of coke and a new ice cream called the 'Extreme' which was delicious. It was a great opportunity to sit round chatting about school.

 I hope you are well and are enjoying your new job. Mum told us that you are now working for a computer company and travelling a lot. Mum hopes we will be able to come and see you at the end of the month during half term. Will you be at home that week or working away? I am really looking forward to seeing you again.

Thank you again.

Love from,

Aaron

Kim loves receiving presents through the post. She writes a thank you to her grandpa.

 Now write a long letter to your aunt, uncle, brother, sister, mum or dad – for a present they have given you.

Dear Grandpa,

Thank you so much for the birthday present you sent me, which arrived by Parcel Force this morning. It was so exciting unwrapping that big box. The gift wrap was beautiful tied up in shiny ribbon. It was such a surprise too. You really shouldn't have spent such a lot of money. Mum says that you spoil me.

An Apple Mac notebook is just what I wanted because I'll be able to use it to do my homework, receive e-mails and search the web. Also, I will be able to get in touch with my friends and follow the movements of my favourite celebrity on the web. It will be useful because my teacher is always asking us to research information. Sometimes we have to type out our homework and send it by e-mail.

When you come and see us, I'll show you how it works. We will be able to sit down together all afternoon and play with it. Then we'll go to your favourite café in the shopping centre where we'll have a café latte because I know that's your favourite drink. Thank you again Grandpa.

With love from your grandaughter,

Kim

Alex loves meeting new people and making new friends.
Write a letter to your new neighbours welcoming them to your street. Fill in the gaps using your own ideas.

34 Birdsong Close,
North Rushford,
RU15 3FT.

Dear Lloyd family,

I have been given your name by our neighbours who are moving to Edinburgh on 15th July, because Mr Lloyd has a new job. I was very excited when they told me they had sold their house to a new family with ten year old twins, who are the same age as me. Let me introduce myself. I am a girl called *(fill in the missing information)* …, I am … , with … eyes and … hair. I live at …, with my Mum who is … and my Dad who is a teacher and leaves for work early in the morning. I have 2 brothers who are called Harry and Jack, who are aged 5 and 7.

You will find that it is a very friendly neighbourhood. There are several children from the street who attend Rushford Community School. Will you be going there? It is an excellent school. I am in Mrs Barker's class. She is … , but gets really angry when you forget to do your homework. My favourite subject is … because …. Every year we have …, when we ….

… is a good place to live because there is a lot going on. We are quite near to the park where you can picnic in the summer or walk by the river. I like to feed the ducks. It's cool. Sometimes we have a drink at the little café by the… Then there is the local leisure centre, which is only a ten minute walk and which has a swimming pool and lots of clubs that you can join – including diving, aqua sports and tennis.

You will enjoy living in Rushford. I am really looking forward to meeting you, as I am sure we will be close friends. Of course I will miss Mr and Mrs Lloyd and their cute kitten Molly, but we are planning to visit them in Scotland next month.

See you soon,

Alexandra

We love going abroad. Write a letter telling somebody about a holiday in a far away place. Finish the letter. Fill in the gaps using your own ideas.

34 Fairholme Road,
Rushford,
RU67 3TP

Dear ....,

You will never guess where I have been for the last two weeks. I've been on holiday in .... staying at…............................... with .... We stayed at the .... hotel, which is .... because it has .... Our room was ....

I've had a wonderful time exploring the beach .... I have been snorkelling in .... and photographed marine life under the water.

My family visited .... where we saw .... The weather was ....
In the evening we ate local food in restaurants including ....

The worst thing about the holiday was ....

There was a thunderstorm that went on all night. It kept us awake because the noise was so loud. The rain fell down. Next morning there were lots of branches in the river.

I will tell you more when ....
Send my best wishes to your family.

Love from,

....

Revise formal letters

* Make a list of formal words or phrases.

* **Think of someone who has a problem**. For example, a teenager.
* **What is his or her complaint?** For example, he or she buys a t-shirt which is very bad quality.
* **Jot down some evidence.** For example,
- it's got a hole in it
- it's too small for the size
* **Jot down a comment.**
- I would like a refund because the quality is so bad.
- I would not have expected this from your shop.

Your turn to write

                                                                                          Your address
                                                                                                       Date

Address of shop

Dear Sir or Madam,

I recently bought a .... from your store at .....
When I unwrapped it at home, I found the quality was ....
I returned it to your store requesting a replacement or a refund, but you refused to give one, saying it must be sent back ....
....

Here are some reasons why I think it is not worth the money I paid for it. It has ....
....
....
....

Your company has a good reputation and has been serving customers for many years, so I am disappointed that you are selling me clothes that are faulty. I would like a full refund because ....

I look forward to hearing from you.
Yours faithfully,

....

Use more _connectives_... link ideas
Use them at the beginning of sentences and paragraphs.

as a result	the reason for this	first	meanwhile
until then	to begin with	finally	this is because
earlier	on the other hand	yet	because of this
as a consequence	at the same time	later	then
just then	consequently	therefore	the next thing
it could mean	it might mean	it may mean	before
although	nevertheless	therefore	suddenly
eventually	in the end	afterwards	as
since	whereas	however	in contrast
contrastingly	which mirrors	in a similar way	despite
even though	so	whilst	but

Common _metaphors_ and _similes_ show how we feel...

He was over the moon with happiness   He was as brown as a berry

Remember _connectives_ that link ideas in sentences are _conjunctions_.

A journey I will always remember

- Lost in the mountains….
- Brakes fail in the car…
- Rough crossing by boat/ turbulent flight…
- Caught up in a plane with hijackers/ terrorists on board…
- You recognise a famous 'terrorist'/ criminal on your plane…
- What do you do?

A day I will never forget.

- A change in time…
- A change in place…
- Wake up in another period of history/universe/future…
- Times have changed as an old man tells his story…

Hidden places

- Secret cave…
- Fairies at the bottom of my garden…
- Through the wardrobe/pond…
- Secret passage in my old manor house leads to…
- Secret treasure…
- A huge room of toys/ computers…

A holiday by the sea

- In the Antarctic, sunbathe on ice not sand…
- See penguins/ polar bears, not seagulls - rent igloo as apartment…
- Hunting/ catching fish for dinner
- Freezing cold

    Things happen on holiday:
- Food poisoning/ sunburn
- Hotel not built
- Meet a shark while swimming
- Float out to sea on inflatable

The creepy house

- Haunted house
- Your parents told you not to go there but you go in and all sorts of misfortunes befall you

New school

- Bullied…
- Bad teacher…
- Put in the wrong class…
- Alone with no friends but someone helps you…
- Evil head teacher is mean to children and does terrible things…

Every story needs a title. Can you give titles to the stories in this book? Here are some more titles. (Each title is underlined.) Each has a list of ideas and can be turned into a story.

Now write the stories.

A big disappointment

- Looked forward to your birthday but everyone forgot
- You get no presents or you don't get what you wanted
- You can't go on holiday and have to stay with relatives
- You come back early from holiday for some reason

Lost

- Lost plane crashes
- Stranded on a desert island
- Dad gets lost driving on a holiday/ to a party
- Lost on the way back from school
- Lost your dog/ cat/ tooth/ race/ toy/ precious item

Babysitting or pet minding for the day

- Looking after a wild animal like a tiger - a friend's naughty dog but it bites and chews and doesn't sleep or eat - a police dog who finds some packages and stolen goods hidden in your garden that you did not put there

- Looking after an animal you are terrified of: a spider or snake

A huge relief

- A trip to the dentist to remove your tooth

- During a display of birds of prey at the local zoo, a bird flies off and you have to coax it back

- A lion…monkey….escapes…

- You have been trapped in a hole/ dungeon/ imprisoned in a castle (you could be a character from history)…but you manage to escape

- You are cut off by the tide/ lost on the moor but you survive and are rescued

- Your ship is sinking or you are crossing the sea in a terrible storm. You think your ship will go down because cups, plates and bottles are crashing down and the lights go off.

- Your plane is in an electric storm/ high wind/ you have turbulence, there is a rough landing

A royal visit to my house

- The queen proves to be human and plays games
- The queen visits your house by mistake, you try to entertain her but it goes horribly wrong

A family day out

- a trip to the zoo goes horribly wrong
- you are accused of trying to steal the crown jewels at The Tower of London
- trip to the moon

A nightmare

- Stranded on a desert island, captured by pirates
- A nightmare - stuck in a castle tower trying to escape and facing some spooky beings
- Left 'home alone'
- Through a painting or wardrobe door
- Going back in time and living with the people of that time

I'll remember that day…

- You get lost in the snow/ fog/ mountains/ wood
- Can't find your way home
- Cut off by the tide
- A trip to the moon
- A trip into space
- Buying a puppy
- Encounter with aliens

My naughty pet

- your pet gets lost
- a stray (lost) cat wanders in through your door. It decides to stay but your own cat is very jealous
- your pet rabbit is a 'house bunny' but he eats all the plants and bites through cables

Look before you leap

- you say arrogantly (boastfully) that you can do something, without thinking
- you have to face the consequences of your mistake (you do a jump off on a horse and fall)

The day everything changed

- You stepped out of your bed onto your blue carpet and it turned into an ocean (stranded in the sea) your pillow is a (boat) a piece of shipwreck, you set out on a adventure.
- At ten o'clock your house goes back in time.
- Car breaks down.
- Mum thinks you're a boy (girl) and sends you to school dressed the wrong way.
- The teacher is in a bad mood, you lose your homework, fail an exam, get punished and stay for a detention.
- Room turns into a rain forest/ a desert.
- Wake in a different place - age - in the 18th century - in the future and aliens take over.
- Put in prison but you've done nothing wrong.

Guinea Pig Education can help you use **punctuation** in *your* writing.

Let's **get going!**

First, don't forget to **write in sentences**. Use **capital letters** and **full stops**.

Jules belongs to **S**ydney at 12 **O**live **G**rove, **R**ushford.

Now try this one:

lois and lulu belong to anya at 14 chesterfield gardens rushford

Use a **!**

That's exciting!
What a surprise!
Oh bother!

Use a **?**

What do guinea pigs eat?

Hold out a piece of vegetable. Will your guinea pig eat it?

Now try this one:

guinea pigs like to be stroked do they bite they are timid but rarely bite ouch

Do not forget to use "**.....**" when you use **direct speech**,

"Anya, what did you buy at the pet shop?" said Jules.
"I bought a cage, some straw, some hay, a bowl, a water bottle and some food for my new guinea pigs."

Use commas for **Lists**.

Use commas **before or after** a **phrase** or subordinate **clause** in a sentence.

Use commas **round a clause hidden** in the **middle of a complex sentence.**

Try these:

Lois is lively inquisitive and nosy

Guinea pigs can be chocolate black silver white and tortoise shell.

My guinea pig called Jules has long hair.

After cleaning the cage Anya put in some hay.

Try these: *(answers on next page)*

What is your guinea pig like anya

Lulu has a white coat, uneven coloured spots and black ears she replied

After running in the grass Jules dozed in his hutch.

Guinea Pigs in the wild live in a burrow.

Some guinea pigs with long hair have rosettes.

Let's remember **apostrophes**:

> The carrot belonging to Jules is **Jule's carrot.**

> The hutch of Lois and Lulu is the **guinea pigs' hutch.**

Plus, remember apostrophes for shortened words.

> They are gorgeous
> **They're** gorgeous

Try these:

> The guinea pig belongs to Kate.

> The hutch of the rabbits George and Ginger.

> Isnt he sweet.

Finally, you can use a **colon** in a list.

> Jess had five smart guinea pigs: a short haired coat, a long coarse coat, a deep shining coat, a smooth coat and one with rosettes and twirls.

Or you can use a **semi colon** to separate two similar ideas in a list.

> Guinea pigs are sociable; they like company.

Try this:
> The male guinea pig is a boar the female is a sow.

Make a sentence with a :
Make a sentence with a ;

For extra information you may need to use a **dash** for a longer pause.

> Dad bought Anya a guinea pig - it was so sweet.

> Jules nibbled his carrot loudly - crunch, crunch, crunch.

Or you could use **brackets** for extra information.

> The guinea pigs (Lois and Lulu) scampered across the grass.

Try these:

> Anya fed her guinea pig he was hungry.

> The rabbits George and Ginger are great friends.

How did you get on?

- Lois and Lulu belong to Anya at 14 Chesterfield Gardens, Rushford.
- Guinea pigs like to be stroked. Do they bite? They are timid but rarely bite. Ouch!
- Lois is lively, inquisitive and nosy.
- Guinea pigs can be chocolate, black, silver, white and tortoise shell.
- My guinea pig, called Jules, has long hair.
- After cleaning the cage, Anya put in some hay.
- "What is your guinea pig like Anya?"
  "Lulu has a white coat, uneven coloured spots and black ears," she replied.
- After running in the grass, Jules dozed in his hutch.
- Guinea pigs, in the wild, live in a burrow.
- Some guinea pigs, with long hair, have rosettes.
- Kate's guinea pig/ the rabbits' hutch/ Isn't he sweet.
- Anya fed her guinea pig - he was hungry.
- The rabbits (George and Ginger) are great friends.
- The male guinea pig is a boar; the female is a sow.

Guinea Pig **Spelling** *Tips*

Guinea pig says, "Don't forget it is important to read through your writing, so you can spot any obvious mistakes. Here are a few basic spelling tips. Make sure you can spell all the words on these pages."

Tricky homophones

Homophones sound the same but are spelt differently.

I gave **two** carrots **to** Jules
But he's getting **too** fat.

Our guinea pigs **are** cute.

They're over **there** by **their** hutch.

Difficult Endings

Some words have tricky endings.

The **latch** on Jules's **hutch** comes open. He gets out and eats a **patch** of grass by the **hedge**. I try to **catch** him but he **dodges** me and runs off.

When I **handle** my little piggy, I **cuddle** him.

Some words have spelling rules.

You double the final letter of a verb with a short sound.

I **hug** Jules.
I am **hugging** him.

I **pat** the rabbit.
I am **patting** him.

I **grab** him.
I am **grabbing** hold of him.

He **hops**.
He is **hopping**.

If the final letter is a consonant, just add the ending.

He **licks**.
He is **licking**.

He **fights**.
He is **fighting**.

I **hold** him.
I am **holding** him.

Drop the 'e' if you are adding an ending with a vowel.

I **love** my guinea pig.
I am **loving** him.

I **stroke** my guinea pig.
I am **stroking** him.

He is having an **adventure**.
He is **adventurous**.

Use the same rule for:

shine   shiny
noise   noisy

But, if the ending begins with a consonant you keep the 'e':

live   lively

love   lovely

lone   lonely

safe   safely

When you add an ending some words change the 'y' to an 'i':

My guinea pig is **happy**.
He is **happier**.
He is the **happiest**.

busy   busier   busiest
cry   cries   cried
piggy   piggies
carry   carries   carried

	Comparative	Superlative
He is fast.	faster	the fastest
He is fine.	finer	the finest
He is a beauty.	more beautiful	most beautiful

Use Sounds

ch, sh, wh, th, oo, ee, ar, or, ur, ir, er, e, ai, ay, oi, oy, oa, ow, ou, au, aw, ce, ci, cy, ge, gi, gy, short y, long y, magic e...

... to sound out 80% of words.

Use syllable to sound out hard words.

Eat **VEG ET ABLES**
Soft 'g' - ge, gi, gy.

are **COM FORT ABLE**

like **MIX TURE**

have an **AD VEN TURE**

SEV EN

PRECIOUS

CREATURE

Remember:

1. Sound hard words out using syllables.

2. Jot down words you find difficult. Learn them.

3. Use a dictionary or thesaurus.

Don't forget to keep your writing neat. Small letters should be the same height. There should be one little finger space between each word.

Make sure you can write this passage:

My guinea pigs feed on green leaves. They munch, crunch, scratch, scrunch in their hutch. Early in the morning it is necessary to feed them healthy food and fill up the water container. My noisy young pigs enjoy playing excitedly in their run on the lawn, where they are safe from danger.

Really tricky ones:

'i' before 'e' except after 'c' - when the sound is ee.

believe

fierce

field

conceited

Exceptions:

neighbour

Silent Letters:

Guinea Pigs:

gnaw

clim**b**

eat crum**b**s

are caut**i**ous

are ca**l**m

are **k**nowing

wrinkle up their noses

Tricky words:

Are you **tough enough** to keep a guinea pig?

They can't be **caught**.

They fill one with **laughter**.

They love to be **photographed**.

Guinea pig says, "Make lists of tricky words you find difficult from the groups of words."

The glossary

A starting point:	is something that gives you an idea to write a story.
The genre is:	the type of story you choose to write. It could be a traditional tale that has a message that good overcomes evil or a romance, horror, fantasy, mystery, realistic or adventure story.
Planning a story:	Structuring the story into three or more paragraphs – with a beginning, a middle and an ending.
Characters:	are people who feature in the story – we learn how they behave and about their feelings, motives, emotions and conflicts.
A setting:	is the place where the story takes place - creating a mood.
The Plot:	is a sequence of events that make up the story. Action in the story may be triggered by a conflict, complication, problem, or unexpected event that needs to be solved.
Suspense:	is built up to leave the reader guessing what will happen. Use: • short sentences for impact – 'Help!' • show the feelings of the characters – 'suddenly his heart missed a beat' – to build up a dramatic climax that leaves the reader on the edge of his chair wondering how it will end.
First person:	tells the story, using 'I' or 'we' – so the reader can imagine being the main character.
Second person:	uses 'you' and speaks directly to the reader or involves the reader.
Third person:	uses 'he', 'she', 'it', 'they' to tell the story as a narrator, like a fly on the wall watching.
Atmosphere:	is the mood and feeling conjured up in the story.
Flashback :	if you start your story with action, you may include few details about what went on before.
Ending or resolution	may be happy, sad, moral (a lesson learnt) or a cliff hanger - where the reader imagines his or her own ending.

Paragraphs:	start a new line (one finger space in for handwriting). Use a new paragraph if you change event, time or place.
Connectives:	are linking words that start paragraphs or join sentences. Examples are: as, since, because, but, if, then, so, as a result of, for instance, yet, after a while, suddenly.
Dialogue:	is what people say and can move the story on. Use correct punctuation – *Lilly said, "Is it hot in here?"* (**direct speech**); *Lilly said that it was hot in here.* (**indirect or reported speech**)
The opening:	is the first sentence of a story - fiction or narrative.
A topic sentence:	is the first sentence in a paragraph, which tells the reader what it will be about. Further sentences will develop the idea and explain it.
Describe:	is making a word picture.
Adjective and noun:	*shimmering sand* (**describing word, naming word**)
Verb and adverb:	*shouting noisily* (**action word, describes action word**)
Powerful verbs and adverbs:	Choosing key words – *'a voice sounded mysteriously'*, *'he nodded his head anxiously'*.
Similes:	compare using as and like – *'as white as snow'*
Metaphors:	compare two similar things, but don't use like or as. *'The dog was a little monster.'*
Script:	tells a story through the characters' dialogue.
Writers' techniques	include: 　* repetition 　* rhetorical questions - questions that don't need an answer 　* personification - giving an object human qualities 　* onomatopoeia - words that sound like their name 　* alliteration - several words that start with the same letter
Fiction:	includes story and narrative.
Non-fiction:	includes information, diaries, leaflets, reports, recounts, descriptions.
Purpose:	why it is written – to inform, explain, describe, persuade, advise or argue.
Target audience:	are the people the article is written for – to instruct someone on how to use a …, to explain how to get somewhere, to persuade or convince the reader to do something

www.ingramcontent.com/pod-product-compliance
Lightning Source LLC
Chambersburg PA
CBHW050715090526
44587CB00019B/3385